The
Dewey Color System® for Relationships

ALSO BY DEWEY SADKA

The Dewey Color System®

The
Dewey Color System®
for Relationships

THE ULTIMATE COMPATIBILITY TEST FOR

LOVE, FRIENDSHIP, AND CAREER SUCCESS

DEWEY SADKA

THREE RIVERS PRESS • NEW YORK

Portions of this work previously appeared in *The Dewey Color System*
by Dewey Sadka, published by Three Rivers Press, an imprint of the Crown
Publishing Group, a division of Random House, Inc., New York, in 2004.

Library of Congress Cataloging-in-Publication Data
Sadka, Dewey.
The Dewey Color System for relationships : the ultimate compatibility test for
love, friendship, and career success / Dewey Sadka.—1st ed.
1. Dewey Color System.   2. Typology (Psychology)
3. Interpersonal relations.   I. Title.
BF698.8.D49S23 2005
155.2'84—dc22   2005014566

ISBN-13: 978-1-4000-5063-5
ISBN-10: 1-4000-5063-4

Printed in the United States of America

Design by Robert Bull

10 9 8 7 6 5 4 3 2 1

First Edition

In memory of my mom,
Louise Moses Sadka

Never insincere, never mean,
always loving and so it seems,
never apart from my heart.

CONTENTS

PART ONE

THE DEWEY COLOR SYSTEM®

Self-Truth: Discover It Together

CHAPTER ONE

What Is the Dewey Color System®?

What lies behind us and what lies before us are tiny matters, compared to what lies within us.

—RALPH WALDO EMERSON

What if there was a personality test you could take in less than a minute? A test so easy even a child could understand it? And what if this test could teach you not only about yourself but also about how you interact in your relationships?

Well, now we have it! The Dewey Color System is the world's only validated personality-testing instrument that is based on color instead of language. It is the first system to scientifically predict the recognized major psychometric personality factors—your traits and motivators—without relying on lengthy, imprecise questionnaires. The Dewey Color System uses your color preferences to quickly reveal the *real* you—not who you believe yourself to be.

LANGUAGE-BASED TESTS ARE IMPRECISE

Since the beginning of civilization, we have labored to discover the hidden motivations behind our actions. Early attempts to categorize and uncover our real selves focused on external influences like the stars, fate, or the elements. This emphasis gave rise to folklore, witchcraft, astrology, and many other systems that are still popular today. In the modern era, investigators started to look at the individual and free will. Gradually, empiricism paved the way for psychology and the analysis of human behavior.

However, one thing has stymied all of these self-discovery systems—the imprecision of language. Consider how each person, asked a particular question, may interpret it differently. Or how stress, fatigue, environment, prejudice, bias, and education can skew test results. Many times people also deceive themselves and fail to answer questions with complete honesty. These are all reasons why experts have longed to create a language-free system to tell us about individual identity.

WHY I CREATED THE DEWEY COLOR SYSTEM®

Working in the staffing-services business for more than twenty-four years, I learned how thousands of people react during periods of crisis. After many years of observing others, I found that often I could predict people's actions and the eventual outcome of particular situations. This inspired me to look for patterns of human behavior that would tend to repeat themselves. My goal was to gain a more objective view of the needs of others and myself.

Since I believe that people are successful when they do what they enjoy, I began searching for a simple key to better understand the desires, concerns, different perspectives, and passions of those individuals who would determine my future. My experiences with traditional personality evaluations, such as the well-known Myers-Briggs testing tool, led me to conclude that they only scratched the surface of understanding an individual. I knew that if I could invent an evaluation that revealed the motivating factors of each person, productivity, sales, and employee morale would surely soar.

With the help of leading academic scholars, I evaluated my concept using a rigorous test of well over five thousand color profiles that took eleven years to develop. Through extensive testing we have scientifically verified the link between color and emotion that many of us already knew existed.

Chemists and biologists use color to diagnose predictable occurrences. For example, biologists can analyze bacteria's red color growth to establish patterns that tend to repeat under certain conditions. Now the same color-based methodology can be used scientifically to identify patterns in human behavior.

The Dewey Color System allows you to learn about yourself without feeling the pain of personally invasive questions. Don't let the fact that it's so easy discount the truth of this new system. Visit deweycolorsystem.com to learn more about how it evolved.

HOW THE TEST WORKS

The Dewey Color System is based on a ranking of your favorite and least favorite colors in four different color categories: primary, secondary, achromatic, and intermediate. Simply put, your subconscious mind is attracted to the colors that indicate your passionate pursuits and not attracted to colors that highlight issues you tend to avoid.

This test also indicates, using only color preference, your

one-of-a-kind connection. In reading about your interpersonal chemistry, you will recognize the gifts that you give each other each day as well as where to best give support.

Why Vibrant Colors Are Best

In constructing the Dewey Color System, we used the spectrum's most brilliant colors, because studies have proved the more vibrant the color, the more distinct the response. This approach ensured a more accurate system that yielded easily measurable results. In fact, an additional scientific study proved that each hue in the Dewey Color System has a physical quality that both of you react to as a unique personal experience.

Color hue clarity was achieved by using pure shades of blue, red, and yellow. For example, our shade of blue contains no red or yellow. Other color blends were meticulously calculated to ensure hue distinction. Black, white, and brown were also added. This process was how we achieved distinctive, different responses to each color vibration in order to capture your core essence.

Proven Reliability

The Dewey Color System is now the world's first and only validated personality-testing instrument based on color. Sixteen personality factors, including the five global factors of Independence, Anxiety, Self-Control, Extraversion, and Tough-Mindedness, can now be statistically predicted by color preference.

The accuracy of my patented system has been validated against two of America's most respected testing instruments— the Strong Interest Inventory, which measures occupational and career interests, and the 16PF, which measures business and clinical aptitudes. Visit deweycolorsystem.com to read more about our landmark statistical correlations and to see scientific journal publications, all compiled by the internationally renowned psychologist Dr. Rense Lange, Dr. Michael McIntyre, research professor at the University of Tennessee, and Dr. Yu-Sheng Hsu, professor of statistics at Georgia State University.

WHAT CAN THE DEWEY COLOR SYSTEM® DO FOR ME?

The Dewey Color System® reveals the chasm between your vision of yourself and others' vision of you. The results of a clinical comparison of my system with the Myers-Briggs, the 16PF, and the Strong Interest Inventory indicated the following:

- Two out of three participants believed that the Dewey Color System gave them a stronger awareness of themselves.
- Three out of four participants believed that the Dewey Color System better described how they live their lives.

Use *The Dewey Color System® for Relationships* to build profiles that you can share with your partner to understand why the two of you interact in a certain way. As you read about how your unique color pairings relate, you will recognize how you and your partner complement each other yet sometimes clash—those absurd attempts to rationalize or suppress the qualities that make you both so wonderful. And by accessing the other's core self, both of you will rise above preconceived notions to honor your own unique relationship.

CHAPTER TWO

Choosing Your Colors

There is more hunger for love and appreciation in this world than for bread.

—MOTHER TERESA

Each of us lives to express a sense of purpose—his or her own individual self-truth. Nowhere is this more apparent than in our relationships. Opposites attract, and yet ironically the same personality traits that bring us together often cause conflict! Consider the following questions posed by frustrated clients: "Dewey, why doesn't my husband listen to me?" "Why can't my wife just relax and trust me?" "My coworker's a great friend, but how can I motivate her to do her job?" "Why can't my child be more patient?" With the assistance of color alone, you'll get beyond irritable quirks and frustrations and thereby gain an instant in-depth awareness of the gifts that you give each other every day.

In my first book, *The Dewey Color System®: Choose Your Colors, Change Your Life,* I wrote about how your favorite and least favorite colors can enable you as an individual to discover your self-truth, your hopes, and your aspirations. In *The Dewey Color System® for Relationships,* I will show you how your and your partner's different personality types mix and match. Whether you are romantic partners, friends, family members, or workplace colleagues, you can learn together how to support each other while remaining true to yourself.

This book explains more than one hundred different color types and offers over five hundred tips for all kinds of relationships. Simply select your favorite colors, and you're on your way to understanding your interpersonal chemistry! Your color choices will guide you toward effective communication at work, a more fulfilling love life, and a closer connection with family and friends.

The test is simple—you can take it in less than a minute!—and you'll simplify your life by reading about the unique connection between you and your partner. There is nothing to fear; no choice is right or wrong. But the ease is deceptive—your color choices reveal a comprehensive personality analysis. Experience together, as millions already have, how living with the Dewey Color System can help your relationships change for the better.

CELEBRATE YOUR DIFFERENCES

What makes your partner tick? Soon you'll be able to understand—and even appreciate!—each other's genuine concerns and behaviors. Often we inadvertently project our insecurities onto those closest to us. Mistaken impressions create negative thoughts, which usually manifest themselves as arguments. This book will show you how not to take your partner's actions personally and instead embrace what makes your relationship special. Many times your partner's "annoying behaviors" are simply the result of his or her efforts to help!

Laugh together about how you keep each other's strengths in check. Reminisce about your shared successes and celebrate triumphant moments together. And rejoice in the discovery that your partner's issues and even contributions are more about him or her than about you. Once you understand each other's self-truth, everything becomes easier. Getting beyond appearances allows each of you to hear the other out.

Friends and Family

Are you bogged down by the irritable quirks of a friend or family member? Learn how to defuse these little things that drive you crazy to create a joyful home.

Romance and Dating

Has fun flirting dissolved into bickering and competitive, combative showdowns? Use the Dewey Color System to rediscover the qualities that brought you together in the first place. Your color choices can make the love last by revealing what's sexy about both of you and how each captivates the other.

Workplace

Do you silently fume over office politics? Understanding how you and your colleagues relate at work can turn frequent disagreements into strengths. Build powerful leadership skills by using color to motivate others and make the most of your natural talents and theirs.

> *The best and most beautiful things in the world cannot be seen, nor touched . . . but are felt in the heart.*
> —HELEN KELLER

CHANGE YOUR POINT OF VIEW, NOT YOURSELF

Learning about self-truth gives both you and your partner the power to be yourselves, even when each feels the need to please someone else. It becomes easier to see other people's point of view, to comprehend their passions, dreams, and fears, which will lead to more meaningful conversations. Unlock your own self-truth and give others the best of you—patient, enthusiastic support.

> *We see things not as they are, but as we are.*
> —H. M. TOMLINSON

HOW TO USE THE DEWEY COLOR SYSTEM® FOR RELATIONSHIPS: FOUR EASY STEPS

Step #1: Self-Truth—Discover It Together

First, turn to the color blocks following page 24 and select your favorite, second favorite, and least favorite color within the primary, secondary, and achromatic categories. Next, choose your favorite intermediate color in each of the three color boxes. Write them down in the "My Color Categories" chart for easy reference (see page 16). Then ask your family member, friend, romantic partner, or coworker to do the same and write their choices down on the Relationships Color Categories page (see page 17).

Step #2: What Your Colors Say About You

Then combine your primary and secondary choices, and turn to your and your partner's personalized color chapters. (For instance, if your favorite primary and secondary choices are red and purple, turn to Chapter 11 to read about how you interact in relationships.) Here is a listing of all the primary and secondary combinations and their personalized color chapters:

Chapter 4	"Yellow and Green: The Caretakers"
Chapter 5	"Yellow and Purple: The Catalysts"
Chapter 6	"Yellow and Orange: The Technical Thinkers"
Chapter 7	"Blue and Green: The Anchors"
Chapter 8	"Blue and Purple: The Thinkers"
Chapter 9	"Blue and Orange: The Builders"
Chapter 10	"Red and Green: The Resource Managers"
Chapter 11	"Red and Purple: The Synthesizers"
Chapter 12	"Red and Orange: The Humanitarians"

Next, add your favorite achromatic color (black, white, or brown) selection to reveal your intimate, romantic connection and workplace relationship chemistry. (For example, if you are a red-purple and add white as your achromatic selection, after you read about your connection to family and friends, turn to the red-purple-white profile later in your personalized color chapter to read about your romantic and workplace connections.)

Note: You can turn to the color blocks following page 24 and pick your colors right now, or read through the rest of Part One if you'd like to gain more background on the Dewey Color System before you begin your journey.

After you review your own personalized color chapter, turn to your partner's and read about his or her choices.

Step #3: What Your Colors Say About Your Relationships

Chapters 13 through 16 focus on your one-of-a-kind inter-personal chemistry with friends, family, romantic partners, coworkers, even your boss. Simply compare your ranking of color choices to your partner's to see how you relate. (For example, if your primary selection is yellow 1st choice, blue 2nd choice, and red 3rd choice, and your partner's is red 1st choice, blue 2nd choice, and yellow 3rd choice, read the descriptions for yellow 1st meets red 1st, blue 2nd meets blue 2nd, and red 3rd meets yellow 3rd to understand your primary connection.)

Chapter 13	"Primary Connection: Your Basic Motivators"
Chapter 14	"Secondary Connection: How You Relate"
Chapter 15	"Achromatic Connection: Your Hopes and Fears"
Chapter 16	"Intermediate Connection: Taking on the World"

Step #4: Creating One Vision through Color

In Chapter 17, "Color by Color," you and your partner can use the color summaries and stories about how others have benefited from the Dewey Color System to experience the empowering simplicity of your self-truths together.

PICK YOUR COLORS

You are about to begin a quest that will deepen your understanding of yourself and intensify your passion for life. Be prepared to view a new, yet somehow familiar, perspective of who you are, who your partner is, what you both say and do, and why.

FREQUENTLY ASKED QUESTIONS

Can I Make a Mistake?

It's unlikely that you'll choose a color that's not meant for you. How can you not choose what you already instinctively know?

However, if the personality descriptions based on the colors you initially choose seem to be off the mark, read about the other colors, and see which apply the most to you. Then choose your colors again. Could it be that you are avoiding your basic self?

If you have a strong reaction to the color description, good or bad, you've probably picked the right color. You tend to feel indifference when reading about your incorrect colors. If you're someone who works with colors a lot, such as a painter or a graphic designer, it can be especially difficult to make your selection.

If you feel that your description was once accurate but no longer reflects who you are, your colors might be revealing your core-personality responses, not your actions. Training and experience have taught you lessons that allow you to change the way you act. When you get upset, though, you need to struggle to keep this core part of yourself from taking over.

What If I'm Color-Blind?

The system is still functional. It will just take you longer to make your choices. So, take your time. Generally, you will dislike the colors you cannot see. You will have an emotional need to learn and express what these color areas represent.

Will My Colors Change?

You bet! When your life changes, so can your colors. Leaving home, getting married, having children, losing someone close to you—all of these events can change your color preferences. For the most part, however, your colors change in varying degrees and not as dramatically as you might think.

Primary favorite colors change when you are questioning your life goals. This change can make you highly uncomfortable with your future. If your least favorite primary color changes, you are probably in a highly reactive period of your life: don't make any rash decisions.

Secondary favorite colors change when you are going through a tough period in your relationship or stretching yourself to connect to others in new ways. If your least favorite secondary color changes abruptly, you have learned a great but hard lesson from one of your relationships.

Achromatic favorite colors change when you are questioning the very core of your existence and feeling indecisive, as if you are on shaky ground. A change in your least favorite achromatic color shows you are reevaluating your entire perspective on life. These changes are temporary. They give you the ability to gather more information, but make the tough decisions more difficult.

Intermediate colors change more than any of the other colors. When your goals change, your color choices often change, too. Get really mad or really happy, and you'll see an immediate change in your intermediate-color preferences. For the most part, however, your favorite and least favorite intermediate colors remain constant.

What If I Like All the Colors?

If you are someone who loves color, selecting a preferred color can be difficult. Artists, designers, and others who have everyday contact with color might have to go back and pick again to be certain. Take a few extra minutes. Eliminate your thoughts about how you use color—make it all about you.

What If I Can't Choose between Two Colors?

Go ahead. Dig deep and pick one. Later, read about the meaning of both colors. One color probably represents who you are and the other one is probably who you feel you need to be. Are you going through a transitional period?

GET READY!

- There are no right or wrong choices—only your choices.
- Your choices aren't about what "looks good" on you or your sofa. They're about what you're naturally attracted to, what makes you feel good.
- Don't rush. Feel the colors. Let them pick you!

Turn to the color blocks following page 24 to make your color selections.

My Color Categories			
Color category selections:			
CATEGORY	FIRST CHOICE	SECOND CHOICE	THIRD CHOICE
PRIMARY			
SECONDARY			
ACHROMATIC			
CATEGORY	BOX 1 First Choice	BOX 2 First Choice	BOX 3 First Choice
INTERMEDIATE			

OTHERS' COLOR CHOICES

Now get friends, family members, romantic partners, colleagues, and even your boss to take the test. Everyone will have fun. If you're not comfortable asking them, leave the color insert open on a coffee table or your desk. Chances are they will pick it up and let you know their favorites without your having to say a word! Then look up your color profiles to find your supportive, romantic, and team-building tips.

Space is provided in this section and at the back of the book for you to record the colors of friends and loved ones (see "Additional Color Pages," pages 221–22).

Relationships Color Categories		
Name		
COLOR CATEGORY SELECTIONS:		
CATEGORY	FIRST CHOICE	SECOND CHOICE	THIRD CHOICE
PRIMARY			
SECONDARY			
ACHROMATIC			
CATEGORY	BOX 1 First Choice	BOX 2 First Choice	BOX 3 First Choice
INTERMEDIATE			
Name			
COLOR CATEGORY SELECTIONS:		
CATEGORY	FIRST CHOICE	SECOND CHOICE	THIRD CHOICE
PRIMARY			
SECONDARY			
ACHROMATIC			
CATEGORY	BOX 1 First Choice	BOX 2 First Choice	BOX 3 First Choice
INTERMEDIATE			
Name			
COLOR CATEGORY SELECTIONS:		
CATEGORY	FIRST CHOICE	SECOND CHOICE	THIRD CHOICE
PRIMARY			
SECONDARY			
ACHROMATIC			
CATEGORY	BOX 1 First Choice	BOX 2 First Choice	BOX 3 First Choice
INTERMEDIATE			

CHAPTER THREE

Celebrating Your Relationships

All colors are the friends of their neighbors and the lovers of their opposites.

—Marc Chagall

Create your one-of-a-kind relationship by mixing, matching, and blending your color selections with those of your partner. With more than five hundred tips for friends, family, romance, and the workplace to choose from, you will discover empowering ways to open others' hearts and minds.

Your first-choice color represents your hopes and aspirations, the ideals you pursue with passion. You will uncover your partner's pillar of strength and determine how you can work together to channel frustrations into positive actions. Check out the tips in Chapters 4 through 12 on color combinations: they will tell you when your companion's sensitivity is heightened and how to avoid a crisis.

Your second-choice color naturally calms down passionate expectations and allows you to command a stabilized, centered perspective. Chapters 13 through 15 explore how reasonable thoughts create levelheaded plans to make frustrations more manageable.

Your third-choice color highlights what's most exciting about you, as well as unfulfilled concerns that consume you when you are upset. Throughout the book, tips will guide both of you toward empowering possibilities on these deeply emotional responses. They will evoke calming truths and keep the two of you in sync.

What Is the Most Popular Color?

We asked more than three thousand people to rank colors from the most popular to the least popular. Here are the results:

PRIMARY CATEGORY		ACTIVE INTERMEDIATE CATEGORY	
1st	Blue	1st	Indigo
2nd	Red	2nd	Lime Green
3rd	Yellow	3rd	Red-Orange
SECONDARY CATEGORY		THINKING INTERMEDIATE CATEGORY	
1st	Purple	1st	Teal
2nd	Green	2nd	Magenta
3rd	Orange	3rd	Gold
ACHROMATIC CATEGORY			
1st	Black		
2nd	White		
3rd	Brown		

YOUR PERSONALITY IS A COMBINATION OF COLORS

As you read, keep in mind that each color category is a layer that acts autonomously, as if the others don't exist. Primary colors are your basic motivators—the fuel in your engine. Secondary colors show how you relate and process your thoughts about others. Achromatics, or noncolors, explain your core being—your hopes and fears. Intermediates expose how you take on the world.

> *As you explore your color preferences, remember that the personalities of both you and your partner reflect a combination of colors, not just a single color.*

COLOR UNLOCKS YOUR MOST INTIMATE THOUGHTS

Each color represents a personal value you need to honor. Your color selections reveal the rewards and consequences of how you prioritize your life. Use the color interpretations in the Dewey Color System to embrace the passions within yourself, to respect the motivations of those you love, and to electrify your life. You will gain the courage and confidence to do what you do best.

YOUR COLOR CONNECTION: A MIX OR A MATCH?

If Your Color Choices Are the Same, You're in Sync

Sharing the same color, a match, creates an unspoken bond. Together you electrify each other's passions and self-confidence. At times, however, you remind each other of past disappointments, struggles, or issues that need to be addressed.

> *The vices we scoff at in others, laugh at us within ourselves.*
> —THOMAS BROWN

If Your Color Choices Are Different, You Complement Each Other

Selecting different colors, a mix, opens doors. Just by being your-selves, you teach each other better ways to achieve goals, under-stand the world, and make decisions.

The more you dislike a color that your partner prefers, the stronger the emotional bond, and the more interesting or sexier the connection. At times, however, you clash with imposing questions that wound egos and make both of you feel alone.

IS THERE MORE THAN ONE "YOU"?

Certain color combinations have one personality at work and another in their personal relationships. If you are one of these combinations, you will finally understand the duality of your dynamic personality.

If you choose these favorite primary and secondary combinations—yellow and purple, blue and orange, or red and green—you'll be asked to select another color to understand the romantic you. For example, if you choose red and green, you'll be asked to select again among these color choices: yellow, blue, purple, and orange. If you select purple, you relate to others as a red-purple. In essence, you become a *purple* instead of a *green* in relationships.

Your original primary and secondary combinations represent your family and friends connection. Your new combination reflects your more intimate, roman-tic side.

If you select brown as your favorite achromatic color, you'll also be asked to choose again to under-stand your more intimate, romantic side. So, if you choose red, purple, and brown, you'll be asked, "Do you prefer black or white?" If you prefer white, you're a red-purple-white. Then you'll read your romance tips, in the "Red and Purple" chapter, for red-purple-white.

Brown represents that neutral space within you where you assemble facts. Your preference of black or white indicates your commitment style in personal relationships.

KNOWLEDGE IS POWER

Sharing this book with the people in your life will have many positive, life-altering benefits.

USE #1: GET TO KNOW YOURSELF

It's just not enough to passionately say, "I want this." Knowing *why* you want something gives you the clarity to keep your invested concerns on track.

Use the Dewey Color System to uncover your self-truth. Celebrate that part of you that you never want to change, and everything will begin to flow: love, wisdom, strength, happiness, and serenity.

USE #2: SUPPORT FRIENDS AND FAMILY

Celebrate the gifts you receive each day from your mom, dad, brothers, sisters, children, grandchildren, and the family that you've adopted—your friends. As you read about others' passions and fears, you'll experience how to best support and fully appreciate your loved ones' heartfelt contributions.

Children are great with colors. Not nearly as bewildered by choice as adults, they select their colors quickly and with remarkable self-assuredness.

> *Unlike grown-ups,*
> *children have little need to deceive themselves.*
> —GOETHE

If you have young children over four years old, the Dewey Color System will aid you in enhancing their self-esteem. Once you understand your children's passions, you'll gain the power to better support them without destroying their essence.

USE #3: SPARK A MORE INTIMATE LOVE LIFE

Your romantic partner—and you—will come alive. Pretensions fade as you become more comfortable in your own skin and begin to realize that the better you know your partner, the closer and more passionate you'll become. Remember the magical moments when you first met as together you mix and match your colors to create your unique chemistry.

USE #4: BUILD A TEAM AT WORK

Discover the workplace style of your colleagues and boss, and learn how to capitalize on your natural strengths and theirs. The workday will go more smoothly as costly misunderstandings diminish and meetings become less stressful. Strengthen your communications together and a build a bottom-line, results-oriented team.

As you read, use *The Dewey Color System® for Relationships* to make your life together an expression of both partners. By honoring each other's self-truths, your journey together will become a joyful celebration. Even new acquaintances will feel as if they have known you for quite a while.

PRIMARY CATEGORY
Select your first, second, and third favorite

Yellow

Blue

Red

SECONDARY CATEGORY
Select your first, second, and third favorite

Green

Purple

Orange

ACHROMATIC CATEGORY
Select your first, second, and third favorite

Black

White

Brown

INTERMEDIATE CATEGORY
Select the color that you prefer in each box

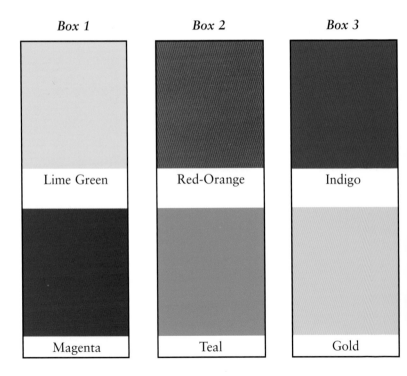

Box 1	*Box 2*	*Box 3*
Lime Green	Red-Orange	Indigo
Magenta	Teal	Gold

PART TWO

FAVORITES

What Your Colors Say about You

CHAPTER FOUR

Yellow and Green

The Caretakers

Yellow-greens have a realistic perspective on life that creates comfortable and secure environments for themselves and their family and friends. You carefully listen to what others say and try to see things from their point of view. By questioning what's really needed, you become more realistic and adapt better ways to manage and direct your day-to-day routines.

FAMILY AND FRIENDS

Your Greatest Contribution

If you love yellow and green: Taking care of family and friends is your purpose and natural talent. No one else does it quite so thoroughly. This is your great contribution. You're the ultimate caretaker. Concerns about your parent's health, your child's acceptance by peers, or a friend's selfish spouse consume your thoughts each day. You see exactly what's bothering them, often before they even have a clue! When you're overprotective, though, you're not doing them any favors. You hate to see anyone in trouble, especially loved ones, but know that it's okay if they fail, because only then will they be able to distinguish what they ought to be doing.

How to Celebrate a Yellow-Green

If your friend or family member loves yellow and green: Pay attention, since it can be hard to detect what a yellow-green really needs. In fact, dedication to you makes it difficult for him to know what's best for himself. Support your caretaker by not allowing him to constantly rescue you or other people. Otherwise, he will spend too much time on everyone else's issues and forget about his own needs.

Encourage him instead to put aside concerns about people and situations for the moment in order to decipher what's most essential to him. Surprise him with favors, such as cleaning the kitchen or planning a special event in his honor. A little help will go a long way. This will also allow you to give back the endearing support he deserves. Your connection will flourish as long as you make sure that he doesn't neglect his own happiness.

Parenting

If your child loves yellow and green: Your child has diplomatic communication skills, which she lovingly uses to help others. Give her duties. Stimulate your child with questions about what would make Mom's or Dad's life easier. Taking care of others is how she learns about the world. Being considerate to siblings, being responsible with chores and toys, and attempting to consult with you about issues are common characteristics of this very grounded child. She readily sees your point of view. Make sure you see hers by asking questions like "How can we make your room more comfortable?" or "What do you really want to do?"

> *Now add your favorite achromatic selection (black, white, or brown) to your primary and secondary color choices to determine your energy type.*

YELLOW, GREEN, AND BLACK

ROMANCE

What's Sexy About You

If you love yellow, green, and black: You are the ultimate confidante and committed partner. Your concerned romantic style stirs the pot and gets things roaring. When others first meet you, they don't have a clue about who you are. Your active listening skills make you very charming. You stun your companion with blunt truths about himself. You tell him about the consequences of saying too much or having unreasonable expectations. For you, speaking the truth is all about being there for the other person—you aim to please. Your intense, protective, high-energy persona is a turn-on. With your honest and undeniable dedication, you create an old-fashioned love-is-forever connection.

Keeping It Hot

You love a good cause and you usually find one in your loved one. But he may feel as though you're criticizing him. Prior to giving advice, consider whether your partner is in a frame of mind to listen. If not, stop talking. Make a mental note and try having the conversation at another time, using a less emotional way of making your point.

If you chose blue as your least favorite primary color: Your dedication to supporting your loved one is unparalleled. With your partner, you're constantly making sure that things are going well. But be cautious. Your honesty, at times, can bruise your romantic partner's feelings. Some things are better left unsaid. Your love relationship flourishes as together you constantly improve the day-to-day quality of your lives.

If you chose red as your least favorite primary color: You want respect. When you meet someone new, at first you're shy, but then you suddenly reveal yourself as a strong, opinionated person that he or she had no idea existed. You are a character! In dating, especially, this quality can be a shocker. Even though you're always truthful, make sure your demands are well thought out. Don't be overly sensitive if your loved one frowns at your remarks. At your best you create clever ways to move your relationship forward without upsetting the status quo.

How to Captivate a Yellow-Green-Black

If your romantic partner loves yellow, green, and black: Your companion is dedicated to you, though it may not always seem that way. Appreciate his blunt comments as gifts—it's his way of showing you love. It can be hard at times to see his true nature. If he misinterprets a situation or an issue, give him more information. He really is all about making you happy. So, celebrate each concern and treasure his advice. By doing this, you create a bond that transforms each day into a playful adventure.

WORKPLACE

Your Key to Success

If you love yellow, green, and black: You are able to be focused and resourceful at the same time. By maintaining a keen awareness of what's going on around you, you always know what's working. This is your great talent. You see true worth and the bottom-line value in every action. At work, you speak out on issues that can interfere with success. When the going gets tough, your steady focus reminds everyone of what's vital. Once your mind is made up about something, there is nothing that can stop you from achieving your goals.

Investing in You

You need to be respected as an authority at whatever you do. Use your directness to educate people on how to better perform their jobs and to increase productivity. When others realize you have their best interests at heart, they will respect your talents. You're at your best when you're advising others.

Careers in fields such as residential architecture, real estate, medicine, or counseling will make you feel more complete. A word of caution: concentrate on building a rapport with others, instead of dwelling on how you are different. Others will feel more secure with your advice and you'll be better able to understand your off-and-on patterns of intense feelings.

How to Motivate a Yellow-Green-Black

If your colleague loves yellow, green, and black: Your strong-willed coworker has the uncanny ability to see what's occurring at such depth that he can monitor your progress, keep you on track like a compass, and make you a winner. When his frankness bruises your ego or disrupts your focus, back off. Unfortunately, he's usually right! Instead of getting defensive and trying to protect yourself, heed your coworker's productive, action-altering advice. Turn his ability to call it as he sees it into a cash cow to benefit your company. If you embrace your colleague's point of view, you will find a real friend who you can trust.

YELLOW, GREEN, AND WHITE

ROMANCE

What's Sexy About You

If you love yellow, green, and white: You instinctively know how to make your romantic partner's life comfortable, whether that means purchasing a comfy new chair for the living room or taking care of his health. Even when your partner doesn't realize it, you see beyond his troubles and stubborn ways to understand what's needed. Your reality-based awareness of others and surroundings allows you to assemble better support structures. By constantly considering new ways to make your lives together a comfortable, enriching experience, you make a house a home.

Keeping It Hot

You are a flexible, considerate, sensitive lover who will not rest until you know that your significant other is okay. Make sure you tell him what you need. Otherwise, you may feel as though you're doing for everyone else and getting nothing back.

If you chose blue as your least favorite primary color: Your emotional commitment to your romantic partner pulls your life together. You have an amazing ability to create a protective family environment. This is your great contribution. Take the time to appreciate what you've learned together each day. Discuss it. Write it down. You will see how you are progressing in your relationship. Sharing what's working together will bring you closer.

If you chose red as your least favorite primary color: Your lack of directness can hide the real you, making it very difficult for even your romantic partner to know how to support you. Your charm will not diminish when you tell him what you need. In fact, showing your vulnerability is very sexy. It will make him feel more important—closer to you.

How to Captivate a Yellow-Green-White

If your romantic partner loves yellow, green, and white: Give your loved one the ability to be himself in an environment with fewer restrictions. He knows how to make the way you live more comfortable, even when you don't. Letting him be free to offer advice without facing criticism will charm him. He will feel a burst of personal freedom and become closer to you. This caretaker knows your mood, even when you're not listening. So, honor him in your thoughts and respect his point of view, and he will respond with sincere love and appreciation.

WORKPLACE

Your Key to Success

If you love yellow, green, and white: You are the best at recommending how to make products, systems, services, or environments fit others' needs. The suggestions that you tact-fully present actually make others feel more comfortable in their own skin. When they hear your concerns, they realize better ways to take care of themselves. Your ability to make fact-based suggestions is your greatest talent. Even in the most difficult situations, when others aren't in the mood to hear, you enable them to appreciate different perspectives and new approaches.

Investing in You

Your communication skills are a tremendous asset in today's workplace. Your ability to understand others' perspectives, adopt their viewpoint, and express your thoughts diplomatically is powerful.

Interior decorating, real estate, career counseling, com-puter programming, travel planning, or any job where you can recommend how to construct a more supportive world works best for you. A word of caution: too many rules or too many opinions render you powerless. Assembling better support structures or making living situations more comfortable then becomes a near-impossible task.

How to Motivate a Yellow-Green-White

If your colleague loves yellow, green, and white: Ask your coworker how you can support him and then listen carefully. This is not someone who is going to pour his heart out to you. Get your colleague to be more specific about his own goals. He needs you and everyone else to do what he asks. Don't worry: a little advice will go a long way. Take advantage of your coworker's ability to be flexible as situations evolve. Ask yourself how you can adapt to his style without disrupting your own goals or creating new dilemmas. He will teach you to become more open to change by understanding others' points of view, and you will be better able to achieve your own goals.

YELLOW, GREEN, AND BROWN

ROMANCE

What's Sexy About You

If you love yellow, green, and brown: You just can't do enough for your romantic partner. Your grounding, healing, supportive insights make his life work. In fact, you experience his needs so deeply that you become part of his own psyche. This makes it easy for you to create nurturing environments where together you can live more in the moment and feel more alive. You are the great giver. A word of caution: if you feel selfish, chances are you're in an unsupportive relationship. Get tough. Learn to distance yourself from people who only want to take advantage of your generosity. Otherwise, you will burn out and hide all the love and concern that you have to give.

Keeping It Hot

To understand the more intimate you, select another achromatic color. Do you prefer black or white? After you've selected your preference, turn to the appropriate page to read your personalized love tips.

If you prefer black, you're a yellow-green-black (see page 29). If you prefer white, you're a yellow-green-white (see page 32). You shift your concerns to become intimate.

WORKPLACE

Your Key to Success

If you love yellow, green, and brown: Your highly realistic perspectives ground everyone around you. No one knows better than you do how to get the most from each workday. You're on a mission to learn how to improve everyone's life. In recognizing and studying others' actions, you see what's necessary for them to do to reach the top. Then, without holding anything back, you give them your much-needed advice. This is your greatest talent. Your quiet strength allows others to trust you and to reveal feelings outside the workplace.

Investing in You

Your dedication to each task allows you to direct and focus your energy. Action-oriented jobs where you can be an expert—doctor, nurse, physical therapist, fitness trainer, or chiropractor—are the ones you would most enjoy. Areas that take advantage of your sharp awareness, like creating products for the home, or your concern for others, like training or supporting a person or system, will fuel your passions as well.

The more you're needed, the more fun your job will be. A word of caution: show your colleagues how much you do. Your hard work must command respect. Otherwise, you become defensive and feel like a victim.

How to Motivate a Yellow-Green-Brown

If your colleague loves yellow, green, and brown: This kind soul just can't do enough for you. Honor his gifts with sincere appreciation. When your coworker is feeling unappreciated, he acts tough or despondent. Coach him to stay focused on his own goals instead of helping everyone else. Pay attention to his recommendations. His realistic, grounding facts will make your workday go smoothly. If you make a point of telling your colleague and others how his valuable perspectives have affected the bottom line, he will be a dedicated team player.

CHAPTER FIVE

Yellow and Purple

The Catalysts

Yellow-purples are on a journey to discover their unique passion for life. Change fuels your inner fire. After experiencing a new environment, you then stand back and analyze it. This sparks your interests. You see the value of each moment and have fun when you're committed to making a difference.

FAMILY AND FRIENDS

Your Greatest Contribution

If you love yellow and purple: Your innate knowledge of spiritual truths inspires others to discover their own spirituality. Your natural curiosity enhances these intuitive powers. By actively listening, making clever observations, and not being afraid to express your feelings, you help others become self-aware and, in turn, spark their passions. This is your great contribution. Family, friends, and others become better able to initiate positive change in their own lives because of you.

How to Celebrate a Yellow-Purple

If your friend or family member loves yellow and purple: Ask for your yellow-purple's opinions and delight in his uncanny ability to grasp how to best approach others and be heard. No one does this better. When you give your friend or family member feedback about your joyful successes, you not only honor his talented communications skills but also enhance his self-esteem.

Protect your friend or family member from overly rigid or routine environments or he will become obsessed with the need to change everything around him. A mundane home life or repetitive job, for example, can create unexpected mood swings or extreme behavior. You might find your family member dropping out of school, quitting his successful job, or moving to a foreign country! Simply be reassuring and trust your quick-to-learn yellow-purple to make the right move. His passions will soar. You'll also find yourself immediately absorbed into a more real, flexible, fun-filled life.

Parenting

If your child loves yellow and purple: Your high-energy child learns by becoming completely immersed in situations. Experiences give him focus. Teach your child math skills while you're shopping, visit the ocean for a science lesson, or even take him to work with you for a day. Afterward, expect a somewhat more logical, very responsible child to ask loads of pertinent questions.

Now add your favorite achromatic selection (black, white, or brown) to your primary and secondary color choices to determine your energy type.

YELLOW, PURPLE, AND BLACK

ROMANCE

What's Sexy About You

If you love yellow, purple, and black: It's no secret that you want to know the intensity of your partner's feelings for you. Possessions and status symbols are just not your main concern. Togetherness for you is being in a relationship that's continually growing. Your intense need for positive change gets things moving. Lovingly analyze your romantic partner's feelings to envision growth possibilities for both of you. You know how to keep your love life exciting. A word of caution: your preoccupation with moving forward can sometimes actually slow things down. Intensity works better when it is directed outward, not inward.

Keeping It Hot

To understand your energy in a relationship, you need to select another color. Do you prefer blue, red, green, or orange? After you've selected your preference, turn to the appropriate page to read your personalized love tips.

If you prefer blue, you're a blue–purple–black (see page 71); red, you're a red–purple–black (see page 100); green, you're a yellow–green–black (see page 29); orange, you're a yellow-orange-black (see page 50).

WORKPLACE

Your Key to Success

If you love yellow, purple, and black: Without even knowing it, you help others make each workday an expression of themselves. You experience their feelings as if they were your own. When coworkers say things with emotion, you become more alert, which allows them to identify, within themselves, their core motivation. You are an inspiration. This is your greatest talent. Others become secure enough to explore their own interests and to recognize worthwhile workplace activities and situations. You give them the inner strength to direct their talents into a work self-portrait.

Investing in You

Your curious personality gives you the opportunity to be an expert in your chosen field. You're at your best when you're learning—asking questions to experience and analyze situations. Knowledge, not money, is your motivation. Doing and experiencing new things means everything to you. And, yes, you are a people person.

Careers that work for you may include family medicine, law, data analysis, social work, and consulting. A word of caution: set emotional boundaries that protect you from becoming too immersed in yourself or in other people's situations. Compulsive concern for others is sometimes a means of avoiding your own issues.

How to Motivate a Yellow-Purple-Black

If your colleague loves yellow, purple, and black: Speak from your heart and give your coworker your full attention. He will hear every issue and internalize its implications. Asking him for advice will fuel his passions. Challenging you to do what's best is your colleague's greatest talent. Don't allow him to become responsible for petty assignments that have little or no significance. It will destroy his motivation. Your coworker's intense, inner-focused energy needs a challenge. So give him one and you'll find yourself immersed in exciting projects that will create amazing things for those around you.

YELLOW, PURPLE, AND WHITE

ROMANCE

What's Sexy About You

If you love yellow, purple, and white: Your joyful, fun approach to everything and everyone makes you quite the romantic catch. New places and constant change are fun for you. Isn't this how you create more passion with your romantic partner as well? At the beginning, everything seems perfect. After a while, though, you start to recognize your true passions. Then you begin to question if you might be happier doing something else or dating someone else. Togetherness for you is an adventurous journey full of new experiences and a strong spiritual connection. A word of caution: forever pondering what you want to do and avoiding commitment can be obstacles to happiness. Don't hem and haw over choices; trust your core beliefs about what would improve things. You already know the answer.

Keeping It Hot

To understand your energy in a relationship, you need to select another color. Do you prefer blue, red, green, or orange? After you've selected your preference, turn to the appropriate page to read your personal love tips.

If you prefer blue, you're a blue-purple-white (see page 75); red, you're a red-purple-white (see page 104); green, you're a yellow-green-white (see page 32); orange, you're a yellow-orange-white (see page 53).

WORKPLACE

Your Key to Success

If you love yellow, purple, and white: You are on a mission to experience life to its fullest. You lift others' spirits effortlessly by telling them the best approach for getting things done. You are an inspiring force that makes respected suggestions on how to improve others' lives. This is your greatest talent. You tell them, for example, how to acquire new accounts or be heard by other employees. Simply by identifying a client's point of view or perspective, you develop strategies that open doors, even those that had already been shut. Use your excellent communication skills to empower others to make their lives more genuine. The world dearly needs people like you.

Investing in You

Your career decisions are based on personal growth. You focus on how much you are going to learn. You prefer nonrepetitive jobs where you are always being asked to seek fresh perspectives. New tasks energize you and reinforce your confidence. You can do almost any job that involves constant change. Fast-growing companies and project-oriented settings where no workday resembles the one before will turn you on.

Careers in corporate communications and marketing or religious occupations enable you to give back, which is your greatest gift. A word of caution: obsessing over what to do with your life can hinder your progress. You can become so busy that you lose your ability to set priorities for yourself.

How to Motivate a Yellow-Purple-White

If your colleague loves yellow, purple, and white: Ask your coworker for his opinion on anything that needs to be communicated with finesse, such as how to break down barriers with a colleague who never joins in. Challenging a yellow-purple-white with strategies on how to best approach someone also fuels his passions: for example, ask for his advice on getting a prospective client to hear your proposal. Trust in his beliefs about what would improve procedures; he's usually right. Your coworker especially needs to respect the people for whom he works. Show your support by giving him unrestricted job responsibilities and backing up his decisions. His powerful communication capacity and uncanny ability to open doors are too vital not to be unleashed.

YELLOW, PURPLE, AND BROWN

ROMANCE

What's Sexy About You

If you love yellow, purple, and brown: The magic of your voice creates a soothing, peaceful aura. It brings out the softer side of your romantic partner. You have a sincere desire for spiritual togetherness in relationships—for someone else to share your life journey. Your spiritual psyche and "can-do" attitude are sexy. Since you're so powerfully aware of your life path, you can find yourself romantically involved with a person who needs your assurance. Be certain that your very special someone gives you spiritual freedom. It will fuel your soul and create a profound, life-altering romance. Avoid suitors who don't appreciate your divine devotion.

Keeping It Hot

To understand your energy in a relationship, you first need to select another color. Do you prefer blue, red, green, or orange? If you prefer blue, you're a blue-purple; red, you're a red-purple; green, you're a yellow-green; orange, you're a yellow-orange.

Now you need to select another achromatic color. Do you prefer black or white? After you've selected your preference, turn to the appropriate page to read your personalized love tips.

If you prefer black, add this new color to what you chose above to become a blue-purple-black (see page 71), red-purple-black (see page 100), yellow-green-black (see page 29), or yellow-orange-black (see page 50). If you prefer white, you become a blue-purple-white (see page 75), red-purple-white (see page 104), yellow-green-white (see page 32), or yellow-orange-white (see page 53).

WORKPLACE

Your Key to Success

If you love yellow, purple, and brown: Your faith puts others on the right path. But your smooth, calming persona can also shock, as you often surprise them with deep insights into their personal lives. With amazing accuracy, you can feel what they need to do, and then tell them how to do it. This is your great talent. Use your unique power to read people to identify fulfilling experiences and encourage others to pursue them. It may be as simple as recognizing who is having fun and who isn't, or asking the right questions to help everyone understand what's going on. You are more aware than most people, so warn others who are in jeopardy of losing sight of their passions, and help them mend things before it's too late.

Investing in You

Choose an environment where you can do your own thing in conjunction with someone else. You gravitate toward people who will teach you through new experiences. You know opportunity when you see it. Unexpected situations are thrilling and enable you to learn how to fit better into the world around you. Consider jobs that bring others back to nature or back to being themselves, such as gardening, flower arranging, massage therapy, or working with others in recovery programs. Your calming voice is a plus in all of these professions.

You will also enjoy high-activity careers where you are part of a team or participate in expansive technologies. A word of caution: appreciate your contributions every day by recognizing what you did to accomplish each task. Otherwise, assignments, projects, and tasks can become difficult to complete.

How to Motivate a Yellow-Purple-Brown

If your colleague loves yellow, purple, and brown: Share your burdens with your coworker. By experiencing them as if they were his own, he will be able to highlight all the benefits of your journey—and even point out how each rift is also a gift. Support your colleague by appreciating his own life journey. Notice how he achieves his results. He lives at such a high volume, chances are you haven't even noticed all his merits. Don't take it personally if your coworker feels your advice is too personal. Bring it up again at another time, when he can hear what you have to say.

CHAPTER SIX

Yellow and Orange

The Technical Thinkers

A yellow-orange's first thoughts are about how to get things done. By establishing a systematic approach, you can figure anything out, from on-the-job tasks to your personal relationships. Your realism makes others see you as technical and efficient. You see yourself, and rightfully so, as someone who makes the most of his or her resources and gets results. You embody the saying "When life gives you lemons, make lemonade."

FAMILY AND FRIENDS

Your Greatest Contribution

If you love yellow and orange: Fun, to you, means being emotionally committed to finding out how all the facts fit together. You examine successful parts of a task or relationship as if you were putting together a puzzle. Each piece is a resource or a personal value that can be used either to make something new or to reinvent a relationship. To the amazement of others, you create something original from what already exists.

How to Celebrate a Yellow-Orange

If your friend or family member loves yellow and orange: Give your resourceful yellow-orange the room to play. He thrives best in a place where stimulating new information can be steadily absorbed. If your friend or family member becomes negative, nitpicking, or overly technical, don't become defensive. He is simply feeling lost and frustrated, searching for where he can be creative.

Give him unrestricted agendas and the time to playfully examine the talents and resources around him. You will benefit as well from his experimental approaches and unexpected, innovative ways. Create passionate adventures together as each of you maximizes the other's resources and talents.

Parenting

If your child loves yellow and orange: Your child demands to play solo—without your input or sibling assistance. In fact, her need to investigate how things fit together can drive you crazy. Don't take it personally. Your yellow-orange learns through touch. Encourage her with games and toys that allow her to build things. Let your child decorate her room. Leave her alone and see how easily she is able to make something from nothing. Bond with your child by celebrating her creativity.

Now add your favorite achromatic selection (black, white, or brown) to your primary and secondary color choices to determine your energy type.

YELLOW, ORANGE, AND BLACK

ROMANCE

What's Sexy About You

If you love yellow, orange, and black: You create nonstop romantic adventures. When you enter a room, your magnetic personality is hard to ignore. Your love of living fast, while slowing down only to listen to your partner, is very sexy. This change in gears helps you get what you want and generates an entirely new view of the world for your romantic partner. Your charge-ahead behavior creates fun experiences in dating and thrilling opportunities for personal togetherness. You are a master at weaving practical realities into an electrifying, emotional connection.

Keeping It Hot

Your lover adores the very inventive and fun you. You can date or marry into what others perceive as a mundane routine and turn it into a party. Togetherness for you is all about inventing an exciting relationship and keeping it going by constantly reinventing it. Creating positive change is your great relationship talent.

If you chose blue as your least favorite primary color: Your commitment to positive change pulls your lives together. But be careful. When your mind races with thoughts about your love life, your on-and-off speeds become irrational barriers—details and feelings that flood your mind. You lose your power to see the big picture. Lead with your heart, especially in dating or in a romantic crisis. Otherwise, others get caught up in your defenses and don't feel your warmth.

If you chose red as your least favorite primary color: You are seeking respect. Though initially you hide who you are, soon others are suddenly confronted by a strong individual they had no idea existed. This can be quite shocking for your dates. For you, being appreciated is a big deal. When your partner frowns or reacts negatively to your boldness, you feel wounded. Try not to take things so personally. Instead, take a break and just wait until he is available to listen.

How to Captivate a Yellow-Orange-Black

If your romantic partner loves yellow, orange, and black: Your high-energy companion needs the freedom to constantly create new and exciting adventures for the two of you. Make some of your routines, especially those without rhyme or reason, available for change. Being too set in your ways can make it almost impossible for your romantic dynamo to be close. Plan fun, new experiences that you both can share. If you feel that your loved one is becoming too intense or brings out his what-you-need-to-do checklist, don't become defensive. His mind is simply overloaded with information and can't think clearly. Slow him down. Get him to talk about what's on his mind. A clear focus will appear and he will adore you for allowing him to draw his own conclusions.

WORKPLACE

Your Key to Success

If you love yellow, orange, and black: One moment you are listening to what others need; the next, you become immersed in solving their problems. You are an innovator, far ahead of anyone else with both people and projects. This is your great talent. You have the ability to create something from nothing by reinventing the resources around you. When you put your mind to something, new ideas and possibilities arrive with a bang. Set your mind and nothing will stop you. Your know-how is unparalleled.

Investing in You

Use your abilities to encourage people and construct new things by pulling together the resources and talents around you. You are a natural at technical work. You're also a great motivator of people. Use both these assets, and you will feel complete.

Your people skills and technical abilities accommodate a wide range of careers, such as selling products that you demonstrate, inventing new products or services that fit into niche markets, or teaching how-to courses. A word of caution: stick longer with what's going well. Constantly reinventing everything and everyone can exhaust your energy.

How to Motivate a Yellow-Orange-Black

If your colleague loves yellow, orange, and black: Motivating this dynamo is easy. Challenge your coworker to invent a new way to market your business, motivate your staff, or make what you do more efficient. Support him by asking him what he thinks. Discussing how your colleague feels about issues will regenerate his more creative side and fuel his passions. You will find yourself working overtime on must-do activities and programs that have inspired you as well.

YELLOW, ORANGE, AND WHITE

ROMANCE

What's Sexy About You

If you love yellow, orange, and white: As a romantic partner, you are the most undefined, lightest combination in the entire color spectrum. Always lighthearted, you bring to each relationship a host of new ways to have fun. When you first meet someone, you mold your behavior to fit him. Becoming part of the situation gives you the information you need to feel close. Afterward, you analyze what's being done, and wonder why it is not approached in another way. Togetherness, for you, is sharing a constant flood of new experiences. Your ideal mate's fixed agendas and routines will actually challenge you.

Keeping It Hot

Your energetic, vivacious, and inquisitive personality keeps things exciting. But don't go overboard. If you talk less, your romantic partner will hear more. Bombarding him with too many agendas will keep him from hearing what's important.

If you chose blue as your least favorite primary color: Your dedication to your romantic partner pulls your life together and helps you see what he needs to improve his life. This is a great talent. Try to be mindful of what you give. Appreciating your unselfish concerns will create an intimate bond you both can share.

If you chose red as your least favorite primary color: You have a great need to be appreciated by your loved one. But don't put on airs to try to impress him. It just makes it more difficult to understand the real you—and that's who he wants to know! Express your heartfelt thoughts with simplicity and sincerity and your loved one will become even closer to you.

How to Captivate a Yellow-Orange-White

If your romantic partner loves yellow, orange, and white: Your fast-moving romantic partner needs your full attention. You can keep him on track by recognizing all the facets of his thoughts, which seem to go on forever. If you actively listen to your companion's never-ending menu of considerations, you will quiet his endless chatter so that he doesn't get lost in his own details. Don't make decisions for your yellow-orange-white or allow him to become overwhelmed with immediate needs. Give this information junkie the freedom to draw his own conclusions. It turns him on. Once a plan is agreed upon, don't let it slip away; keep the enthusiasm high.

WORKPLACE

Your Key to Success

If you love yellow, orange, and white: Your ability to learn quickly and memorize information keeps you on the cutting edge. You love to research everything before making a decision. By sharing what you know you make everyone's life easier. From you, your colleagues learn about the newest resources, pertinent facts, and innovative ways to relieve workday pressures. Your open-minded yet analytical approach opens the doors to profit.

Investing in You

Thanks to your talent for analyzing numbers and information, you're always among the first to know whether or not something will work. You thrive in careers where you can rely on your factual expertise.

Consider working with computers, as a statistician, a reporter, a librarian, or in research. A word of caution: don't make plans and agendas and then fail to act on them. Set goals and stick to them by protecting yourself from outside negative influences.

How to Motivate a Yellow-Orange-White

If your colleague loves yellow, orange, and white: Challenge your coworker with questions about how to best research a project or perform a task. Then listen to his invaluable expertise or instructions. You will discover productive shortcuts and easier ways to get the job done. If you feel that your colleague is becoming too intense and is overloading you with information, support him by asking how each fact will affect the goal. Motivate your coworker to prioritize by encouraging him to clarify his thoughts. With a clear focus, he'll get back on track with a regenerated spirit. Knowing that his suggestions have benefited others makes him more self-assured.

YELLOW, ORANGE, AND BROWN

ROMANCE

What's Sexy About You

If you love yellow, orange, and brown: You make sure that everything is going well for your loved one. Your sharp eye sees all before he has a clue. You build your partner's confidence by reminding him of his strengths. He feels loved and safe with your constant guidance to keep him on track. Your dedicated and committed spirit is sexy. When you lend a helping hand, your down-to-earth advice makes your significant other adore you. A word of caution: don't sound the fire alarm when you intuitively see that your companion's actions are going nowhere. Give him more time. Craft innocent questions that allow him to anticipate the consequences of misguided activities.

Keeping It Hot

To understand the more intimate you, select another achromatic color. Do you prefer black or white? After you've selected your preference, turn to the appropriate page to read your personalized love tips.

If you prefer black, you're a yellow-orange-black (see page 50). If you prefer white, you're a yellow-orange-white (see page 53).

WORKPLACE

Your Key to Success

If you love yellow, orange, and brown: Your dedication to helping others gives you the focus to pull an unraveling situation together. By observing how things work, you recommend more efficient ways of making everyday processes or work routines easier. Fixing things is your great talent. Use your sharp eye to recommend repairs and regenerate fraying relationships among staff. You make work fun—accomplishments become a victory. Your fresh perspectives, high-energy level, and intense living style revive even the dullest moments. Others love to be a part of the passionate world that you inspire.

Investing in You

You clearly understand what others bring to the table. Use your ability to distinguish the doers from the talkers. No matter how hard anyone tries to get the emotional edge on you, it's not going to happen. Use your exactness to ensure that the facts at hand are the primary consideration when making a decision or a deal.

You'll thrive at high-activity or how-to jobs or wherever you can assemble the nuts and bolts in order to fix things or issues. Consider a career in customer service, repairs, administration, product development, or manufacturing. Avoid work environments where you're forced to deal with abstract concepts. A word of caution: guard against becoming too immersed in details. If you lose sight of your objective, you will lose your creativity and yourself.

How to Motivate a Yellow-Orange-Brown

If your colleague loves yellow, orange, and brown: Ask your coworker how to fix something. It's essential that you share all information, even the problems! Once he becomes immersed in your situation, don't react when he sounds the alarm. It's simply your colleague's way of setting priorities. Don't expect an answer right away either, but be assured that he will return— first with numerous questions seeking more information and then with recommendations. Support your coworker by appreciating his sincere advice. Listen as he explains to you, in detail, the significance of each of your actions and demonstrates the most effective way to do something. A simple "thank you" is enough to motivate this very dedicated, knowledgeable, and supportive soul.

CHAPTER SEVEN

Blue and Green
The Anchors

Blue-greens have fun nurturing and supporting others. Your endless curiosity entices people to tell you what they're thinking. You share their dreams and are sensitive to their needs. You give others the self-confidence to believe in their own capabilities. Your honest, sympathetic listening is a stabilizing influence that makes them feel important.

FAMILY AND FRIENDS
Your Greatest Contribution

If you love blue and green: Your sincere concern gives your closest companions the faith to believe in themselves. It also gives them the inner strength to decipher what's best for their future. This is your great contribution. Just being around you gives them the impetus to seek their dreams. They gain the capacity to be comfortable with themselves above all.

How to Celebrate a Blue-Green

If your friend or family member loves blue and green: Your supportive blue-green listens intensely to you. What she needs most is for you to listen to her. Her tone of voice tells all. Let her lead the conversation once in a while and simply encourage her to express her thoughts without sharing any thoughts of your own. Your articulate anchor will try to throw the topic back to you, but be steadfast. Make it all about her. In learning how to meet her needs, you make your life together more pleasing.

When your blue-green becomes too comfortable or too earnest, challenge her with enticing questions about what she expects. For example, ask her what her idea for a perfect day would be, or if she could have anything in world, what would it be? Just ask! She knows what she wants. Otherwise, your friend or family member will neglect her own personal and relationship growth. It is amazingly easy to positively transform a blue-green, even though it appears difficult.

Parenting

If your child loves blue and green: Your child is a sponge. He mirrors you. His endless curiosity hears everything, even your thoughts. Share your dreams—especially those you had at his age. Ask him about his dreams. Stimulate your child by asking for his advice or talking to him as if he were an adult. Intellectual conversations challenge a blue-green.

Now add your favorite achromatic selection (black, white, or brown) to your primary and secondary color choices to determine your energy type.

BLUE, GREEN, AND BLACK

ROMANCE

What's Sexy About You

If you love blue, green, and black: Your attractive appearance and attentive disposition are very alluring. You dote on your romantic partner with sincere, empathic, supportive concerns. Your endearing puppy-dog eyes and tone of voice express real concern. People are magnetically drawn to you. Truly listening to others is your greatest power, and it makes you a natural in relationships. You need to feel what your partner feels—his joy and pain. Shared emotions become treasured justifications that you two exist as one. Your desire to live the romantic dream is sexy.

Keeping It Hot

You are constantly in touch with your romantic partner's emotions and clearly know what he wants. Don't expect the same from him. No one listens as well as you do. Instead, appreciate your gift to make your loved one more aware of the issues that he couldn't confront without you.

If you chose yellow as your least favorite primary color: You see others as they perceive themselves. Beware. In dating, you can attract someone who does not respect your concerns. Get real before you get attached, or you will have never-ending "soap opera" love affairs. In a long-term romance, make sure your expectations are realistic before you set your heart on something. Does it work for both of you? If not, drop it. Don't be so stubborn.

If you chose red as your least favorite primary color: You are very seductive, mysterious, and even flirtatious. Without a hint of what you're up to, your empathy effortlessly attracts whatever you want. However, sometimes you can "hear" way too much information or attract the wrong suitors. Speak up for yourself more. Otherwise, you'll be stuck in relationships that aren't reciprocal.

How to Captivate a Blue-Green-Black

If your romantic partner loves blue, green, and black: Dote on your blue-green-black. What he wants is two-way open communication. Pay attention when your partner speaks, and let him know that his concerns are yours too. Be sincere. He can tell by your voice if you're genuine. If he becomes frustrated, simply ask him how he feels. Listening is all you have to do. He has a real need to be confirmed. If you offer advice, know that he heard you—even though his initial lack of response can make you feel that he didn't. It just takes him longer to process information about his feelings.

WORKPLACE

Your Key to Success

If you love blue, green, and black: You are the great listener. When people speak, you hear their hopes and fears in their voices. Then you talk with them to help them discover what they need. Your genuine empathy for others instills workplace loyalty in your employees: they work for *you,* the boss, not the company. The ability to translate employee needs into support and keep each individual on track is your greatest talent. It allows you to determine your own identity as well.

Investing in You

Being sensitive and supporting your coworkers' emotions is a responsibility that you can rightly claim. If you're a manager, your ability to remain dedicated to your staff will create strong employee commitment and loyalty. Your intensive listening skills make you a valuable coworker, one who can refocus colleagues. Customers and clients love your personal interest in them and trust you with even crucial decisions.

Careers where you can meet and greet the public work best for you: writer, actor, psychologist, psychiatrist, manager or designer of support systems, sales manager, or mechanic. A word of caution: if you get too close to those you work with, you will be unable to give unbiased guidance. You work best in environments where you consistently encounter new clients or situations.

How to Motivate a Blue-Green-Black

If your colleague loves blue, green, and black: After your coworker speaks, repeat what he has said back to him. Let him know you heard everything. Confirm what this blue-green-black does right and let him know how much you appreciate his input. A little feedback will go a long way. As long as you're genuine, your colleague will go out of his way to support you and the company's goals. Don't feel defeated when he appears to "know all the answers." Present your ideas anyway. He will eventually acknowledge your suggestions. It just takes him longer to process information. You will find that he was open-minded about your discussion after all.

BLUE, GREEN, AND WHITE

ROMANCE

What's Sexy About You

If you love blue, green, and white: In dating, others can believe you're unobtainable—the ultimate seduction. But once you are in a relationship, your naturally supportive disposition makes your romantic partner feel that you're genuinely there for him. You anchor your significant other by directing him toward what's needed to balance his life. It's easy for him to hear your straightforward, unbiased comments. Your heartfelt, astute commonsense remarks make him feel closer to you.

Keeping It Hot

You get others interested by giving them your undivided attention. Then you appear unavailable. Some people might find this enticing, but it will be difficult for them to get close to you. This is especially true in dating. Intimacy can make you uncomfortable. You simply require more information about people before you can get close to them.

If you chose yellow as your least favorite primary color: You appear to be very open and endearing. Others may feel that you have a need to be loved, but then you become distant. Explain to your significant other that you need space to clarify your thoughts, especially during a crisis. Be careful. Lead with your heart and keep your concerns focused on those you love.

If you chose red as your least favorite primary color: You are very seductive, mysterious, and flirtatious. You think about how it would feel to be with someone, and this curiosity attracts whoever you want. Others don't have a clue about your thoughts. Don't rush into telling them, either. Your profound considerations take time. Otherwise, you might find yourself in an impulsive relationship. Even after commitment, you will still be curious about all the options available.

How to Captivate a Blue-Green-White

If your romantic partner loves blue, green, and white: Your sexy romantic partner loves the thrill of the chase. So, don't push. When you get too close, he'll feel uncomfortable. If your blue-green–white appears aloof, simply back off. Don't question his loyalty. He's discerning how to best support you or the situation. When this happens, change the subject for a while. Support your partner by honoring the way he keeps his strength. You'll captivate him from afar, and he will treasure and love you even more.

WORKPLACE

Your Key to Success

If you love blue, green, and white: You are an objective manager with astute common sense. Staying objective in difficult situations, when others are losing their cool, gives you the power to recommend solutions. This is your natural talent. You can keep your distance, yet maintain your concern. Coworkers' faith in you motivates you to work even harder. Accept the reality that you are much more than your job. This understanding will open doors and expand your potential. You will maximize your performance in almost any task or profession focused on supporting others.

Investing in You

You are at your best when you can use your influence to recommend easier ways to do things or support others. Seek positions that give you the opportunity to manage people, information, or workplace environments.

Your neutral, not obsessive perspective enables you to teach, to manage, or to work in accounting and auditing, especially at a large corporation. Be proud of your supportive role. Your concern for others and your innate ability to eliminate excesses make you an ideal manager. A word of caution: don't allow unsupportive environments to make you appear remote, cold, or uncaring.

How to Motivate a Blue-Green-White

If your colleague loves blue, green, and white: When your coworker's supportive suggestions keep you from going astray, tell him about it. This blue-green-white will in return constantly let you know when excessive thoughts or expectations are preventing you from moving ahead. You'll motivate him if you appreciate his perspective. Don't assume by his sometimes aloof manner that he doesn't care about you: his distance simply gives you both the insight to know what's best. Remember, his primary concern is to anchor you with solid support. Heed your coworker's advice or expect him to remind you later that you must not have been paying attention.

BLUE, GREEN, AND BROWN

ROMANCE

What's Sexy About You

If you love blue, green, and brown: The sense of personal harmony you receive from being with your romantic partner makes him feel important. Protecting him becomes your mission. Your significant other feels safe as you guide your lives away from extremes to improve situations and find peace. You are totally there for your partner and want to help him make his dreams come true. When you're together, you are both totally relaxed and feel right at home. A word of caution: don't go overboard. When you are first too nice and then too selfish, you make it difficult for your loved one to appreciate all the good you do. Simply be a bit more selfish up front!

Keeping It Hot

To understand the more intimate you, select another achromatic color. Do you prefer black or white? After you've selected your preference, turn to the appropriate page to read your personalized love tips.

If you prefer black, you're a blue-green-black (see page 61). If you prefer white, you're a blue-green-white (see page 64).

WORKPLACE

Your Key to Success

If you love blue, green, and brown: Even when they don't ask, you are able to tell others what they need. Your amazing awareness instantly identifies practical solutions. Issues are more quickly resolved thanks to your realistic approach and clear understanding of what's actually required to complete a task. This is your great talent. Use it to promote sound business practices and positive work environments. You are the dream maker. Everyone benefits from your sound advice, especially you.

Investing in You

Choose careers where you can become immersed in the process of doing something. Your reality-based approach makes things work.

You are at your best when you are either supporting people through crises or fixing things: good career choices for you are doctor, nurse, physical therapist, corporate trainer, chiropractor, forest ranger, or carpenter. You see life from a hands-on, supportive perspective. A word of caution: you can lose yourself in unappreciative environments, so create workplace alliances or choose to work at a company where you will be appreciated for your grounded concerns.

How to Motivate a Blue-Green-Brown

If your colleague loves blue, green, and brown: Honor your coworker's efforts to make your life better by respecting his advice. Heed his warnings, especially when your blue-green-brown repeats them. His concerns are grounded in facts. If you pay attention, even when you think he's wrong, you'll find yourself a winner more often. Your own success fuels his passions; after all, his goal is to make things work. Share your victories with this great protector who will stop at nothing to help you succeed.

CHAPTER EIGHT

Blue and Purple

The Thinkers

Blue-purples are visionaries. You ponder existence. You need to know why things are. The conclusions you reach allow you to see the big picture, in terms of both creating original ideas and improving on the ideas of others. Your focus on the future enables you to live in an optimistic way.

FAMILY AND FRIENDS

Your Greatest Contribution

If you love blue and purple: You are a great motivator. When you question others about what drives them and offer your own insights on getting things done, you challenge them to think. This is your great contribution. You improve the status quo by seeing empowering possibilities within the big picture. Problems are solved and ideas turn into reality.

How to Celebrate a Blue-Purple

If your friend or family member loves blue and purple: Mitigate your thinker's expectations without discouraging his trailblazing ideas. Appreciating his endless stream of big-picture concepts is key. Ask your blue-purple to imagine what can be done about a problem and watch his passions soar. It's how he has fun. But be vigilant. Without steadfast encouragement and advice your blue-purple is prone to worrying. If he fears something has been done for the wrong reason, he can veer off track.

Remind your blue-purple not to think so much; otherwise, his fantasies about doing something new may erode his confidence. Having too many pictures in his head makes life difficult, even impossible. Nothing measures up. Unwittingly, he asks for the unattainable, especially from himself.

Parenting

If your child loves blue and purple: Your mentally demanding, highly imaginative child who lives in a fantasy world needs firm rules or he will make up his own. Keep your child grounded and on track by explaining the *why* behind your advice. He loves to think. Challenge your blue-purple: ask him how he would solve a difficult problem. His conclusions will be stimulating—and they may shock you!

> *Now add your favorite achromatic selection (black, white, or brown) to your primary and secondary color choices to determine your energy type.*

BLUE, PURPLE, AND BLACK

ROMANCE

What's Sexy About You

If you love blue, purple, and black: When you think about your romantic partner's deep emotional concerns, you spark passion. Your constant investigation of feelings, thoughts, and ideas is sexy. When you first meet that special person, you dive in with all your heart. You create a surreal world and put him on a pedestal, as if he were a movie star. He feels your strong desire to be close and trusts you with his most intimate feelings. By understanding his motivation, you create a powerful bond.

Keeping It Hot

Your expectations will never turn out the way you envisioned them. Fantasy is fun, but it can erode your real life. Be pragmatic and realize that *your* thoughts are not always in sync with your partner's. When you feel emotional about something, stop and take a breath. Chances are you're ignoring concrete facts or going down a selfish path that's only about you. Stay grounded and joyful moments will replace your frustrations.

If you chose yellow as your least favorite primary color: Your dramatic, eccentric flair is sexy. Your fast-moving, never boring persona creates exciting adventures. People adore your animated body language—it's entertaining. When you move too fast, however, your connection diminishes. In dating, you will imagine right off the bat that you've met the perfect partner. On reflection, you see the whole person, warts and all. Be more cautious and realistic about people before you get involved. Otherwise, you will be constantly disappointed.

If you chose red as your least favorite primary color: You see each person's depth and possibilities. Your openness to everything makes you very appealing. Your curiosity may be interpreted as a romantic request—it's seductive. People love your fun and easygoing style. Don't be naive or impulsive: others will take advantage of you. This is especially true in dating. Loving and caring about someone does not mean you should ignore your own needs. Make a list of criteria you require to have a fulfilling relationship, and if someone or something falls short, talk about it.

How to Captivate a Blue-Purple-Black

If your romantic partner loves blue, purple, and black: Your blue-purple-black's romantic ideas make the world around him delicious. He wants to be charmed—enveloped—by you. Forget about practical details, especially in the beginning. Have fun. Encourage fantasies. Simply get him to picture an enticing mood, then enjoy it. Your imaginative partner will do the rest. Support him by calming his sometimes overexuberant spirit. Turn him on by keeping him grounded.

WORKPLACE

Your Key to Success

If you love blue, purple, and black: You are the darkest color in the spectrum. Darkness denotes emotional depth. Visualizing possibilities is your greatest talent. Your ability to picture things clearly in your head gives you the capability to perform tasks with very few missteps and minimal risk. Others see this quality as self-confidence. They think you always know what you're doing, even when you don't. Once you understand the overall concept, there's nothing you can't do. Your dramatic flair gives you the power to enlist others in your crusade to initiate innovative products and services. Use it to venture down new paths and create opportunities.

Investing in You

Use your big-picture thinking to develop new markets, new ideas, and new businesses. You see what's missing and know how to get things done. You are a great motivator who needs to make an impact by expressing new ideas.

You will be happiest working in a creative field such as advertising, marketing, sales, design, and trial law, or in any profession that allows you to investigate the unknown. A word of caution: working in environments that encourage questions is vital to your success. Otherwise, you become frustrated and react by doing something that you later regret.

How to Motivate a Blue-Purple-Black

If your colleague loves blue, purple, and black: To get this pioneer to imagine new possibilities, ask him about ideas and then watch him light up. But don't stop there. Play devil's advocate to ensure that your coworker's vision is workable. If you hear a lot of emotion in his voice, ask him to stop and take a breath. Chances are he's ignoring concrete facts, making false assumptions, or harboring unrealistic expectations. Discuss with him why something is being done a certain way or if there's an easier way. Compliment your coworker on his accomplishments. His work energy will zoom if you get him to appreciate the end result, even though it probably isn't exactly what he planned.

BLUE, PURPLE, AND WHITE

ROMANCE

What's Sexy About You

If you love blue, purple, and white: Your very classy style creates dozens of romantic possibilities. When you first meet a person, you have no clue if he is right for you. Your concerned yet objective nature makes you appear unavailable, somewhat regal. You're the ultimate challenge. When people get to know you, they feel your warmth by your very personable questions and sincere concerns. You make them feel as if everything is going well. For you, togetherness means being an integral part of your partner's life. It brings out your best qualities and makes your life exciting. Your romantic illusions keep things spicy.

Keeping It Hot

You constantly mull over what each person or situation requires. During this period, people may view you as passive or quiet, but once you have assembled all the facts about the situation, they meet an exciting, dramatic person who is all about making the relationship fun.

If you chose yellow as your least favorite primary color: Because you need to know all the answers, you may seem unavailable or somewhat formal. Your expectations about how you see yourself in the future may be somewhat unreasonable. Enjoy the present instead of obsessing over the future. Only then will who or what you're looking for appear.

If you chose red as your least favorite primary color: You appear seductive and intriguing and may even evoke a sense of the forbidden. People who meet you will find you very appealing, but may be surprised later on when they see how logical you are. Your outrageous curiosity provokes enticing situations. Take the time to decide exactly what you need, and be specific. Don't let others bully you. You can weave a comprehensive plan on your own that makes everyone happy. Just do it.

How to Captivate a Blue-Purple-White

If your romantic partner loves blue, purple, and white: Wear your favorite dress, create your most alluring look, but don't get too close. For your blue-purple-white, romance is about creating fun illusions. When he appears wishy-washy, encourage him to stay focused, but don't push. External pressure, especially from you, will negatively affect your partner's ability to be intimate. Give him space to make his own decisions. He simply enjoys reviewing all the options. Go on dates that stir the imagination. Ask your partner to plan fun outings or surprise him with the night of his dreams. Announce your intent ahead of time, since diversions captivate him.

WORKPLACE

Your Key to Success

If you love blue, purple, and white: You're the great problem solver. People don't see your talents right away. They often give you a puzzled look as you sit contemplating the big picture. Then you literally lean forward with a host of options to make things work. Your greatest talent is objectively examining ideas and situations and then offering solutions. Without outside interference, you analyze and transform an idea into reality and then critique it until it is perfect.

Investing in You

You're brilliant at organizing, developing, and working with ideas to bring situations, people, or markets together to solve problems. Your original perspective is your greatest strength.

Many career paths are open to you—public relations, human resources, corporate law, architecture, career counseling, marketing, customer service—any profession that needs problem solvers. A word of caution: demand autonomy. External pressure or a boss who forces you to act in a certain way will destroy your creativity. Don't float too many ideas, agendas, or topics. Without firm goals, you lose focus and appear wishy-washy or scatterbrained.

How to Motivate a Blue-Purple-White

If your colleague loves blue, purple, and white: Challenge your coworker to solve a problem, but don't stop there. Bombard him with all the facts—just focus on one topic at a time. Switching topics or discussing two different problems at once can be a disaster. Give your problem-solving colleague time to weigh all the options, resolve difficulties, and make a plan. He functions well under pressure, but sometimes he might need time away from you to sort things out. As long as you stick to the facts and are especially careful to avoid false assumptions, your highly motivated coworker will generate amazing solutions for you.

BLUE, PURPLE, AND BROWN

ROMANCE

What's Sexy About You

If you love blue, purple, and brown: You know exactly how to make your significant other a success—and he loves the way you think. At times, however, he may see you as too direct. Of course, you think you're just relating the "big picture" of what's not working to your partner. Don't take it personally if he's suddenly devastated. Instead, work on crafting more subtle questions that will still make an impact and get your point across. Your comments are invaluable, even if they upset the status quo.

Keeping It Hot

To understand the more intimate you, select another achromatic color. Do you prefer black or white? After you've selected your preference, turn to the appropriate page to read your personalized love tips.

If you prefer black, you're a blue-purple-black (see page 71). If you prefer white, you're a blue-purple-white (see page 75).

WORKPLACE

Your Key to Success

If you love blue, purple, and brown: Like a scientist, you go from idea one moment to measurable result the next. Your greatest talents lie in developing new products, more efficient methods, or practical operational solutions. You have no patience with impractical ideas, either your own or others'. Your very realistic, grounded understanding of things gets the job done. Colleagues see you as an analytical, process-oriented person; they depend on you not only to envision new ideas, products, or ways to do something but also to analyze the viability of your solutions.

Investing in You

There will be no stopping you if you seek out environments that provide plenty of autonomy and appreciate your dedication. Otherwise, you won't be able to stay focused on your long-term goals.

Occupations such as scientific research, acting, quality-control management, product design, and gourmet cooking offer you the best opportunities. A word of caution: others can perceive you as being too direct or abrasive. Ignore them. Tactfully present your facts, as your point of view, and then ask for theirs. Know that your invaluable, fact-based comments will be implemented, maybe just not as fast as you expect.

How to Motivate a Blue-Purple-Brown

If your colleague loves blue, purple, and brown: Simply ask your coworker to identify issues he thinks need to be addressed and watch him get to work. Your blue-purple-brown relishes devising a solution, then evaluating it. In no uncertain terms, he will give back facts and recommendations that make things more efficient. To really fire up your colleague's engine, grant him full ownership of all projects and provide tons of feedback. Keep him motivated by asking his opinion before you implement something new. It will give him owner-ship and you'll become a winner as well. Motivate him by assigning tasks or projects that he can easily monitor to see what's been accomplished.

CHAPTER NINE

Blue and Orange

The Builders

Blue-oranges demand an exciting life and create it with their dual personality. One moment you are an innovative free-thinker who wishes to construct a radical modular home; then you shift gears and become a traditional critic who wonders why anyone would undertake such a lark. Your probing questions spark conversations. This makes you fun at parties. Your friends are a bunch of characters with very diverse interests.

FAMILY AND FRIENDS

Your Greatest Contribution

If you love blue and orange: By analyzing your environment—reducing thoughts and situations to their most basic form and reconstructing their occurrence—you build a better world. This is your great contribution. Sometimes you stop and wonder why you always find yourself in the middle of such craziness. But deep down you know that too much order in a social environment is restrictive.

How to Celebrate a Blue-Orange

If your friend or family member loves blue and orange: Positive change, ignited by wide-ranging conversation and lots of activity, fuels your highly social blue-orange. Social situations that challenge your friend or family member actually serve to strengthen his self-confidence. Don't let him get bored. When a blue-orange is not building something, he becomes frustrated, emotionally depleted, even depressed.

Be loyal to your blue-orange by keeping him foremost in your thoughts. Honor how he treasures you. Support his dedication to different causes; it's what makes him feel most constructive. When your friend or family member becomes fiercely preoccupied with alliances that are going nowhere, help him extricate himself from the situation. But be careful. Don't discourage his sense of purpose—his belief that the world needs him.

Parenting

If your child loves blue and orange: Talk about activity overload! Your very social child demands an exciting life full of action. It's how he learns. Draft a manageable activity plan for him and stick to it. Keep your child busy by reading, or simply stir his imagination about what you are going to do next. Visit construction sites or other places where things are made. Eliminate the chaos by challenging your blue-orange with projects that he'll find interesting, as long as they don't weigh you down.

Now add your favorite achromatic selection (black, white, or brown) to your primary and secondary color choices to determine your energy type.

BLUE, ORANGE, AND BLACK

ROMANCE

What's Sexy About You

If you love blue, orange, and black: Romantically, you are a blast. By constantly appraising past experiences, you know right away who or what is best for you. Your constant barrage of questions keeps expectations realistic. As a result, both you and your partner experience happiness. This is your powerful relationship talent. A word of caution: your intense scrutiny can be misinterpreted as negative or even disloyal. If you slow down a bit, you can keep things on the right course without emotionally wounding your loved one.

Keeping It Hot

To understand your energy in a relationship, you need to select another color. Do you prefer yellow, red, green, or purple? After you've selected your preference, turn to the appropriate page to read your personalized love tips.

If you prefer yellow, you're a yellow-orange-black (see page 50); red, you're a red-orange-black (see page 112); green, you're a blue-green-black (see page 61); purple, you're a blue-purple-black (see page 71).

WORKPLACE

Your Key to Success

If you love blue, orange, and black: You manage expectations or refine procedures by asking pertinent questions. Nothing escapes your sharp eye. Before you break down a product, others' feedback, or difficult issues, you first zero in on what's not significant. Then you pull together viable elements to envision obtainable goals: better ways to build something, utilize resources, or revamp unrealistic budgets. This is your great talent. Use your keen perception to scrutinize tasks and make recommendations for greater efficiency. You have a natural managerial style.

Investing in You

You're a natural both at developing new products or procedures and at delegating tasks. You prefer a busy environment, even if it is stressful, because you enjoy learning. Pressure stimulates you.

Careers that involve managing tasks, overseeing or implementing change, assessing value, and analyzing efficiency are best for you. A word of caution: work for companies that respect your dedication. Does management listen to your concerns? Are loyal employees treated with respect? If the answer is no, move on.

How to Motivate a Blue-Orange-Black

If your colleague loves blue, orange, and black: Honor rather than question your coworker's dedication by including him in operational planning. Expect efficient, process-oriented input that will make your project easier and more cost effective. By involving your coworker in the early stages you give him ownership and fuel his core motivation. But if you notice that he's under pressure, take steps to calm the chaotic activities that he enjoys under normal circumstances. Otherwise, his intense scrutiny will slow him down. When your colleague becomes better able to prioritize plans, he will reward your support with loyalty.

BLUE, ORANGE, AND WHITE

ROMANCE

What's Sexy About You

If you love blue, orange, and white: Romantically, you are an exciting bundle of energy that can't be denied. You constantly examine your loved one's point of view to see the very depths of his motivation. This is how you regularly fine-tune your romantic connection to keep it on track. If you feel that you're being told what to do, you lose your footing. Slow things down, and try not to second-guess yourself. Keep the lines of communication open. Don't end a conversation until your romantic partner gets to have his say. The crazy, fun couple you are will flourish once all the facts are out in the open.

Keeping It Hot

To understand your energy in a relationship, you need to select another color. Do you prefer yellow, red, green, or purple? After you've selected your preference, turn to the appropriate page to read your personalized love tips.

If you prefer yellow, you're a yellow-orange-white (see page 53); red, you're a red-orange-white (see page 115); green, you're a blue-green-white (see page 64); purple, you're a blue-purple-white (see page 75).

WORKPLACE

Your Key to Success

If you love blue, orange, and white: You observe with a sharp eye and effortlessly gauge productivity: just by walking around, you seem to know who is going to accomplish his goals and what project will become a huge success. Your ability to view the marketing of products, ways to improve a design, or operational functions in great detail is amazing. This is your great talent. With your much-needed insight, you can initiate a plan or a new product, critique what's not working, and then offer innovations.

Investing in You

Companies that empower you to construct new things will get you excited. Improving a product, service, or the work process is also a good use of your talents.

Your skill for suggestion is best suited to the hospitality industry, corporate law, resource management, employment recruitment, or the operational areas of companies, where you can decide how to direct resources and people. A word of caution: focus on what you want and stick to it. Becoming distracted or bored is your great weakness. Don't waver, or you'll wind up in a dead-end position.

How to Motivate a Blue-Orange-White

If your colleague loves blue, orange, and white: To keep your coworker on track, get him to set goals periodically and analyze his own productivity. Don't tell him how to do something: simply tell him what you want and to get back to you with a plan. This blue-orange-white is very efficient at inventing process-oriented activities. Giving him the freedom to devise his own plan will make your workdays full of adventure. In a crisis, protect your coworker from an endless cycle of second-guessing by talking through things with him. Otherwise, he'll ultimately talk himself out of exactly what is needed most.

BLUE, ORANGE, AND BROWN

ROMANCE

What's Sexy About You

If you love blue, orange, and brown: Your giving and affectionate nature creates hope. Maybe that's because you're dedicated to making the world a better place. You're not just a talker; you're a person of action. You inject a sense of purpose and caring into your relationship. Be careful, however: don't leave behind your romantic partner while rescuing everyone else. Under pressure, you may do the wrong thing, even though it feels right at the time. If you avoid making rash decisions, you'll be the lovable person that your partner adores, always there to lend a helping hand or give a big teddy-bear hug.

Keeping It Hot

To understand your energy in a relationship, you first need to select another color. Do you prefer yellow, red, green, or purple? If you prefer yellow, you're a yellow-orange; red, you're a red-orange; green, you're a blue-green; purple, you're a blue-purple.

Now you need to select another achromatic color. Do you prefer black or white? After you've selected your preference, turn to the appropriate page to read your personalized love tips.

If you prefer black, add this new color to what you chose above to become a yellow-orange-black (see page 50), red-orange-black (see page 112), blue-green-black (see page 61), or blue-purple-black (see page 71). If you prefer white, you become a yellow-orange-white (see page 53), red-orange-white (see page 115), blue-green-white (see page 64), or blue-purple-white (see page 75).

WORKPLACE

Your Key to Success

If you love blue, orange, and brown: Your can-do attitude gets things done in the most efficient manner. Dedication to those around you challenges you to go beyond what's expected. When you're actually doing something that you planned, your strong beliefs and no-nonsense approach make it happen. This is your greatest talent and can even become your life mission. Your astute awareness is comforting and allows others to believe in you. Look around: doesn't your action persona instill a can-do attitude in others as well?

Investing in You

When you are focused on building something, you're at your best. Occupations that allow you to make direct, exact specifications or careers where you can impact social values by getting others to work better together will fuel your passions.

Careers in engineering, building, and developing new

programs, companies, or products will challenge you. Also consider jobs in fields where you can make a difference, such as law enforcement, firefighting, and social or government work. You need to be involved in lots of activity directed at improving services for those around you in order to feel good about yourself. A word of caution: when you're upset or under pressure, you lose sight of your long-term goals. Avoid making rash decisions. Take a moment to relax and have fun. Your inner strength will return and with it all the plans that you hold so dearly.

How to Motivate a Blue-Orange-Brown

If your colleague loves blue, orange, and brown: His sharp eye sees how to build new things. Don't question your coworker's insight. Just get more information about how to keep it within budget. He's an expert at using resources within the organization, creating efficient programs, and getting donations or sponsors. Give him a cause to fight for and there is no stopping him. Honor your colleague for his process-oriented, grounded awareness and be prepared for an entirely new person to arrive on the scene—one who is fueled with motivation to give you or the organization unrelenting support.

CHAPTER TEN

Red and Green

The Resource Managers

Practical and nurturing, red-greens teach others how to achieve more value in their lives. No one fools you. You're a dynamic personality and know exactly what everyone is up to. You've got a knack for knowing what's important. A natural parent or teacher, you're concerned about how to make people's lives better. Helping others gives you self-respect.

FAMILY AND FRIENDS

Your Greatest Contribution

If you love red and green: You are at your best when you are directing the use of resources. You start out very nurturing but become very authoritative and even bossy. There is no middle ground. You are either one way or the other. This can be confusing to those around you. People don't always realize that even when you're bossy, you're just looking out for their best interests.

How to Celebrate a Red-Green

If your friend or family member loves red and green: Understand that both sides of your dynamic red-green are in full support of you. He knows how to best invest your time and money. Honor his dedication by listening to his advice, even the tough stuff. Your friend or family member's directness is not mean-spirited. In fact, it's all about making your life work.

Constantly worrying over you is a red-green's way of protecting you. If you're feeling distraught, back off. Reappraise the situation. Chances are you have heard something you needed to hear. If he's being overly judgmental, don't take it seriously. It's simply the way he talks to himself. Learn from it. Later, you'll find your red-green open to hearing your thoughts, especially about what you need. Sincerity will go a long way. It gives him the confidence to make your home or friendship together a comfort zone.

Parenting

If your child loves red and green: Your practical, nurturing, amazingly sweet child also shows a bossy side, especially as she gets older. Don't be upset. It's her way of being needed. Your child can manage herself, with your input. Giving orders won't work—expect tantrums. Get really close to her by asking her opinion. Then discuss yours. If you feel the two of you are drifting apart, trouble is brewing. Become your child's best friend by asking her for help. You'll be amazed at her spot-on thoughts and how well she knows you.

Now add your favorite achromatic selection (black, white, or brown) to your primary and secondary color choices to determine your energy type.

RED, GREEN, AND BLACK

ROMANCE

What's Sexy About You

If you love red, green, and black: By focusing on your romantic partner's needs, you learn about situations and issues that are of value. Even when he puts up a fight, your sound advice directs your partner to follow successful paths. Instinctively you know what works best for him. Togetherness for you is all about creating a mutually supportive relationship where you're honored for your kindness, concern, and accomplishments. It turns you on. Being supported by your loved one makes you feel secure and in control of your life. And you know instantly when your significant other is fully supporting you, and when he's not.

A word of caution: you can be judgmental under pressure. When trying to resolve problems, be more fair-minded. Tact wins more respect and support than using an all-or-nothing approach.

Keeping It Hot

To understand your energy in a relationship, you need to select another color. Do you prefer blue, yellow, purple, or orange? After you've selected your preference, turn to the appropriate page to read your personalized love tips.

If you prefer blue, you're a blue-green-black (see page 61); yellow, you're a yellow-green-black (see page 29); purple, you're a red-purple-black (see page 100); orange, you're a red-orange-black (see page 112).

WORKPLACE

Your Key to Success

If you love red, green, and black: You know the value of money and resources, as well as the intrinsic worth of each coworker's contributions. You ask, "How much did you get from what was expended?" and always manage to stay on time and on budget. This is your greatest talent. By being sensitive to how different people express their emotions, you also learn who supports each goal and who does not. You gain the ability to understand others' needs, even when they don't know themselves. Your very presence makes others feel comfortable.

Investing in You

Appreciate your ability to know when support is needed and where money can best be spent. You can excel in careers that place a high emphasis upon the optimal use of resources.

Consider money management (finance, accounting, investment banking), manufacturing, property management, production analysis, consulting, architecture, sales, or teaching. You will do well wherever you can be nurturing and direct. A word of caution: in resolving problems, don't make quick judgments. Take the time to be more fair-minded and you'll see the long-term consequences of each decision.

How to Motivate a Red-Green-Black

If your colleague loves red, green, and black: This strong-willed colleague listens to you in a very supportive way one moment, then tells you what you should have done the next.

Don't get defensive; both sides are in full support of you. Know that he will stop at nothing to keep you focused. It can be frustrating when he obsesses over small matters, but don't allow his judgmental remarks to upset you. This red-green-black will change his mind the next day when you present new information. Be loyal. Don't forget that he's on your side. Your dedication will motivate him to help you in every way possible.

RED, GREEN, AND WHITE

ROMANCE

What's Sexy About You

If you love red, green, and white: You intuitively know how to balance the practical areas of your lives together. Even when you first meet Mr. Right, you keep your cool. You sort out all the facts and put them in order to identify problems and offer never-ending support. This is your great talent. By critically examining all the possibilities just for the two of you, you determine how to best use money and cultivate each other's talents. Your ability to maintain a practical perspective and a sense of adventure creates exciting romantic encounters.

A word of caution: show your sincerity and warmth. Otherwise, your romantic partner may see you as someone who is all about rules and agendas.

Keeping It Hot

To understand your energy in a relationship, you need to select another color. Do you prefer blue, yellow, purple, or orange?

After you've selected your preference, turn to the appropriate page to read your personalized love tips.

If you prefer blue, you're a blue-green-white (see page 64); yellow, you're a yellow-green-white (see page 32); purple, you're a red-purple-white (see page 104); orange, you're a red-orange-white (see page 115).

WORKPLACE

Your Key to Success

If you love red, green, and white: Your objective point of view and practical thoughts and considerations make the best use of all resources. This is your great talent. You have an open-minded approach to tasks that takes into account everyone's talents. Then you critically analyze and reformat things to complete goals. Others have no clue how you so swiftly create practical solutions, and at times neither do you. You have the vision to create positive, visible change in people's lives.

Investing in You

Your logical, supportive perspective is often in demand. You understand the underlying premise of things and work best when challenged by new points of view. Consider environments where you're in constant contact with different types of people or situations.

Careers that involve compiling information, such as training, career development, organization of tasks, auditing, and marketing, will allow you to express your supportive energy. A word of caution: when you're upset, all others see is your critical nature. Step back and assess all the issues, then speak from your heart, not your brain. It will keep your team on board in your behalf.

How to Motivate a Red-Green-White

If your colleague loves red, green, and white: Be open and sincere and this wizard will adopt you as part of his family. Don't let his objective, factual nature turn you off. Look again and you will see a genuine concern behind each comment. Your coworker's knowledgeable sense very clearly sees when you've overstepped your capabilities or even crossed into someone else's business. Stay focused on your responsibilities and he will go to extreme lengths to make each day work best for you. You'd have to search long and far to find a more supportive work colleague.

RED, GREEN, AND BROWN

ROMANCE

What's Sexy About You

If you love red, green, and brown: You bring out the best in your loved one by helping him accept both his limitations and his abilities. Your dedication and support are unrelenting. This generates a powerful physical connection. The two of you become engaged on a crusade to grow together and make your dreams a reality. Being appreciated for your concerns and accomplishments grounds you. A simple thank-you or being told that something you did made a difference is enough for you to stay focused on your loved one's concerns. Your hands-on dedication makes you a powerhouse consumed with protecting your great love.

Keeping It Hot

To understand your energy in a relationship, you first need to select another color. Do you prefer yellow, blue, orange, or purple? If you prefer yellow, you're a yellow-green; blue, you're a blue-green; orange, you're a red-orange; purple, you're a red-purple.

Now you need to select another achromatic color. Do you prefer black or white? After you've selected your preference, turn to the appropriate page to read your personalized love tips.

If you prefer black, add this new color to what you chose above to become a yellow-green-black (see page 29), blue-green-black (see page 61), red-orange-black (see page 112), or red-purple-black (see page 100). If you prefer white, you become a yellow-green-white (see page 32), blue-green-white (see page 64), red-orange-white (see page 115), or red-purple-white (see page 104).

WORKPLACE

Your Key to Success

If you love red, green, and brown: Your nonstop energy is dedicated to making improvements. Once you know what you want, you go for it! Turning everyday needs into a cause to champion is your great talent. When you direct your energy inward, you are a tower of strength; when you turn that energy toward others, you are a giver; and when you turn that energy toward goals, you are a practical director. Others see you as a whirling dervish and sincerely appreciate how you utilize various tools or instruments to give strong, directive support.

Investing in You

Appreciate the power you have, and stay on the lookout for what you and those around you need to be successful. You must feel that what you do somehow provides supportive structures or tools for others.

Hands-on professions in the medical field, such as dentistry, nursing, or surgery, or in the human-resources field, such as teaching or managing, will help you understand yourself better. Also consider physical jobs where you provide emergency support to keep things running well. A word of caution: taking on too many responsibilities can eventually destroy your passion and give you a short fuse. Allow yourself to relax. This will restore your energy and help you bounce back with a renewed, dedicated spirit.

How to Motivate a Red-Green-Brown

If your colleague loves red, green, and brown: This dedicated crusader is looking for a cause and will usually find one in supporting you. His cautious nature makes him a good fit in the business world. If you hear that this coworker has been saying negative things about you, keep in mind that he does respect you and wants you to succeed. Give support by assisting with your colleague's frantic schedule or encouraging him to back off when he becomes carried away with thoughts of supporting others. Be cautious about his efforts to support you: don't pile excessive responsibilities on him. He is a charge-ahead team player who will do everything possible to get the job done.

CHAPTER ELEVEN

Red and Purple

The Synthesizers

When others speak about their foremost concerns, red-purples give them full attention. You walk away remembering what was most important and are better able to prioritize issues or highlight actions that need to be taken. You have a unique ability to put two and two together and come up with a plan for any situation.

FAMILY AND FRIENDS

Your Greatest Contribution

If you love red and purple: When a crisis occurs, you're able to quickly analyze the event, cut out the nonsense, and pull things together. You feel complete when you're giving direct support. You know how to put an end to situations that are interfering with your goals or negatively affecting those you love. Your concerns create a positive, secure world for your family and friends.

How to Celebrate a Red-Purple

If your friend or family member loves red and purple: What a red-purple really needs from you is the permission to pull things together. It's essential. Without the ability to support you, he will become negative or overanalytical. Simply give him the control to direct priorities and in return he will give back unvarnished facts, powerful strategies, supportive suggestions, and workable plans. Everyone benefits when a red-purple's tough side melts. Hardships will become easier to deal with.

Remember, your red-purple is fiercely loyal and will stop at nothing to protect you. No one does this better. His advice comes straight from the heart.

Parenting

If your child loves red and purple: Your red-purple child is loaded with charm and uses it to get his way without asking. Give him control of his room and play area. Honor your child's space and stay very aware of yours. Explain things in steps. What's first? Don't try to fool him—he needs to know the facts. Instead, boost his self-esteem by asking his opinion. You'll be amazed at how he can analyze events and cut out the nonsense.

> *Now add your favorite achromatic selection (black, white, or brown) to your primary and secondary color choices to determine your energy type.*

RED, PURPLE, AND BLACK

ROMANCE

What's Sexy About You

If you love red, purple, and black: By paying close attention to the emotions of those you love, you compel them to express themselves. Your genuine concern makes your significant other feel important. By giving him your full attention, you captivate him—it's very sexy. Togetherness for you is having the capability to create a world where you both can grow and evolve independently, but with support.

Keeping It Hot

You are sexy, seductive, and usually get what you want. But when a relationship comes to an end, you are able to put aside your hopes for that person and move on. You regain a clear understanding of your feelings. When your heart leads, there's no stopping you.

If you chose yellow as your least favorite primary color: You are focused on your love life. Problems occur when you get carried away with supporting the other person and he does not appreciate or respect you. Then there's hell to pay—taking you for granted is a big mistake. But if your expectations make your heart hard, stop. You're asking more than your partner can give. Accept his limitations before you make a judgment. Otherwise, you'll end things before the relationship is really over, and hold a grudge to boot. Give him more time.

If you chose blue as your least favorite primary color: You're well aware of the many factors that can cause a relationship to succeed or fail. Your ability to judge people accurately after first meeting them impresses others and is your great talent. Your dedication to your loved one creates a powerful bond. In a crisis, however, your knowledgeable perspectives and direct, no-holds-barred communications can really wound their egos. Craft a softer approach, before you pounce.

How to Captivate a Red-Purple-Black

If your romantic partner loves red, purple, and black: Be open; tell your partner about your feelings. Discussing matters of the heart fuels his desires and gives him the ability to be close to you. You won't regret it. This dynamo will protect you from outside interference, and in so doing will pull his own life together. Get accustomed to the fact that when you're not prioritizing for *everyone's* benefit, you will hear about it in no uncertain terms. Appreciate even his toughest remarks—it's how your partner shows concern. Protect him by being yourself. Mixed signals can interfere with his ability to support you. Give your loved one the autonomy to set priorities for your life together and he will dedicate himself to you.

WORKPLACE

Your Key to Success

If you love red, purple, and black: Your strong personality directs others to get their priorities in order. When they speak, you sort out the facts from the emotions. Then, thanks to your inexhaustible energy supply, you establish a step-by-step action plan. No one does this better than you. Creating win-win situations is your great talent. Coworkers trust that in your hands projects get done and obstacles are overcome. When you're in charge and feeling good about your future, you are an inspiration to everyone.

Investing in You

You function best in a work environment where you're in control of all the resources you need. Careers in which you have the power to calm those around you by offering quick solutions without issuing blame are best for you. Your understanding of the importance of listening to others' concerns makes you a great motivator—a team builder.

Careers in recruiting, politics, religion, or entertainment will give you a sense of fulfillment. You might even consider being an event planner, an editor, an administrative assistant, or running a business in which you can set all the terms of operation. A word of caution: request the autonomy and time to finish your projects up front, before you get frustrated. Everyone will benefit.

How to Motivate a Red-Purple-Black

If your colleague loves red, purple, and black: Ask your coworker to develop a strategy for you. You'll be amazed at how he gets behind the scenes to unearth forgotten resources or develop a better system by merely changing the order of how things are done. Turn your colleague into a dynamo by giving him control of his immediate space, protecting him from outside interference, and clarifying his responsibilities. Otherwise, he'll lose focus and become unable to do what he does best—prioritize and pull things together. Be on his team and he'll support you in return. Red-purple-blacks have an amazing ability to turn things around when a situation seems like it's going downhill fast.

RED, PURPLE, AND WHITE

ROMANCE

What's Sexy About You

If you love red, purple, and white: When it comes to romance, you're the soothsayer. With your innate ability to know what's coming next (and your natural good sense), you create a safe zone, protecting your loved one from negative out- side influences. Your ideal romantic partner is one who gives you the latitude to determine priorities for both of you. Once given control, you predict your direction. Herein lies your greatest talent. Inside this very private world, where you can both playfully be yourselves, you become very seductive. Togetherness for you is all about being able to guide your romantic partner down paths to where you both can flourish.

Keeping It Hot

Your appearance and the way you dress are very well put together. You're so collected others will wonder where the chaos hides in you. This creates real sexual appeal. You are wary of others until you really get to know them. However, doesn't the unknown arouse you? Some may find it frightening, but for you that's where the fun is.

If you chose yellow as your least favorite primary color: You know how to get the exact type of relationship you want. You also assist others by sharing your knowledge when it comes to affairs of the heart. But make sure you give yourself the *time* to have a relationship. Otherwise, you can suddenly find yourself involved with exactly the kind of person you were avoiding.

If you chose blue as your least favorite primary color: You mentally note each trait that will or will not work when you first meet someone. You're the ultimate matchmaker—for your friends, that is. In fact, others can have a hard time meeting your standards—but why waste your time or theirs? In dating, trying to keep things superficially fun and casual can inadvertently make you appear to be a bit ditzy, and it doesn't get you any closer to finding the love you want. Be yourself. Keep your own dedication strong, and you'll effortlessly achieve the relationship you're seeking.

How to Captivate a Red-Purple-White

If your romantic partner loves red, purple, and white: Togetherness works best when you give your red-purple-white permission to manage the direction of your future. Listen to his warnings. After all, hasn't his thorough analysis of issues in the past been spot-on for the most part? Honor this powerful, concerned way your partner shows love. It comes straight from his heart to protect you. Tell him afterward how much money and time you saved or how you avoided a frustrating situation. It will give him the courage and faith to cement his own objectives— bringing the two of you closer.

WORKPLACE

Your Key to Success

If you love red, purple, and white: You uncover the truth behind sticky situations. Then you contemplate your new information to accurately predict the outcome. This investigative ability is your great talent. Your amazing insight both avoids disasters and creates opportunities. In the workplace, you might be found critiquing the quality of a service, the marketability of a new product, or the usable functions behind a design. You see the facts behind the facts, and in so doing can forecast the profitability of offering a new service or product, or even hiring a new person.

Investing in You

You have the ability to get the job done right the first time. You are at your best when you are advising the people in power. Expending a great deal of focused energy on each activity ensures your success. You know how to cut out unnecessary steps so as not to waste time.

Consider careers in marketing research, data management, forecasting market niches or trends, or wherever you can analyze exactly what's real or applicable to a given situation. A word of caution: your critical skills can limit your future and destroy your best ideas, opportunities, or passions. So be direct with yourself. It will give you the faith and courage to maintain a stronger focus on your objectives.

How to Motivate a Red-Purple-White

If your colleague loves red, purple, and white: Listen to every point your coworker makes. Honor his ability to hear and assess information and you'll become more successful as well. Support him when you feel his critical analysis has turned inward and has made him somewhat overwhelmed, even scatterbrained. Simply get your colleague to talk about his thoughts. You'll hear great ideas, and this red–purple–white will be back on track with a passionate endeavor. Expressing his thoughts gives him the power to guide you away from inaccurate information, costly assumptions, or policies that could incite hostility from fellow employees.

RED, PURPLE, AND BROWN

ROMANCE

What's Sexy About You

If you love red, purple, and brown: Your romantic partner knows all too well that you become the center of attention wherever you go. Your fun, high-energy level is infectious and everyone adores how you spice up their lives. Isn't this also how you boost your own spirits? A word of caution: don't let your great schemes and desires cloud your judgment and keep you from being with the one you most treasure or expressing your softer, more lovable side. When your life feels too intense, slow down or you'll spin your wheels.

Keeping It Hot

To understand the more intimate you, select another achromatic color. Do you prefer black or white? After you've selected your preference, turn to the appropriate page to read your personalized love tips.

If you prefer black, you're a red–purple–black (see page 100). If you prefer white, you're a red–purple–white (see page 104).

WORKPLACE

Your Key to Success

If you love red, purple, and brown: Your natural talents pinpoint what others need to do when they're drifting and clueless. Your grounded comments show others how to come to grips with the reality of their circumstances. This is your great talent. You create bold new solutions to lingering problems. You learn by observing your competitors, then duplicate their achievements for your own use. Your focused, high-energy approach makes quite an impact. Others can't help but pay attention when you cut through the status quo to create new and better ways to get things done.

Investing in You

Focus on careers where you can analyze your environment, see what looks promising, and then pursue it. You can fly solo. It's easy for you to define by yourself what you need to do. Consider using your talents and resources in ways that eclipse conventional practices and expectations.

You're a natural in careers where you can generate enthusiasm for a product or design a better way of doing something (perhaps it's deciphering different ways to manufacture a product, improving services, or fixing complicated mechanisms). A word of caution: when your life feels too hectic, slow down. Your need to get things done can destroy your ability to consider all the facts or present your ideas in a way that you can be heard.

How to Motivate a Red-Purple-Brown

If your colleague loves red, purple, and brown: This powerhouse of energy needs to be constantly recharged. Motivate a red-purple-brown by simply checking with him before you make any changes. He will astound you with his observations. Give your coworker control of your physical surroundings and he will give back to you products, services, or action plans that work. Making practical decisions on your behalf fuels his passions. Support your colleague by keeping his more adventurous schemes and desires from clouding his judgment. You'll find yourself working with a strong, dedicated, supportive, passionate, and somewhat crazy coworker who is going to win or die trying.

CHAPTER TWELVE

Red and Orange

The Humanitarians

Red-oranges love individuality. You believe in walking your own path, standing out from the crowd, and speaking your own mind without apologies. If someone gets out of line, you're not about to keep quiet. You're looking for unconditional love, and hope to create an environment where everyone can express himself without fear of embarrassment. You're concerned that everyone is treated fairly. This is your great contribution. You're one to look people in the eye, and your very presence brings forth a sense of integrity.

FAMILY AND FRIENDS

Your Greatest Contribution

If you love red and orange: You create a very special, intimate connection with your family and friends. Big is not necessarily better for you. Small towns, small gatherings, and small groups of friends hold greater rewards. They allow you to stand out and feel worthwhile. Too many distractions in your social world can create emotional anxiety and eliminate your ability to see the truth.

How to Celebrate a Red-Orange

If your friend or family member loves red and orange: It's hard to find a friend or family member more loyal or protective than a red-orange. All he asks is that you trust him to do the right thing. Where he most needs your support is outside of your network of family and friends. Others can see only a red-orange's directness, without his warmth. Get your friend or family member to open up. Don't allow his need to set boundaries and protect his sensitive side undercut others' appreciation of him.

Support your red-orange by not getting defensive when, ready or not, he tells you what you need to do. Instead, be secure enough with yourself to learn from his factual points. If he becomes upset, you'll know it. Let him vent about things that just aren't working. Later, your friend or family member will be his undeniably lovable self again.

Parenting

If your child loves red and orange: Your very sensitive and outspoken child needs lots of hugs and to hear love in your voice. When you ask him to do something, always speak from your heart or he will physically act up. Honor your child's individuality by avoiding the word *no*. Instead, give him a reason for your refusal: "This won't work for you because . . ." Acknowledge him when he walks into a room. Be sincere when you tell him how much you love him. Motivate your red-orange by spending quality one-on-one time together.

Now add your favorite achromatic selection (black, white, or brown) to your primary and secondary color choices to determine your energy type.

RED, ORANGE, AND BLACK

ROMANCE

What's Sexy About You

If you love red, orange, and black: Even though you sometimes come across as somewhat aloof, you're really a big teddy bear. Once your romantic partner has connected with the endearing you, it's hard to turn him away. You are there, on your partner's behalf, making sure his contributions are respected. Small gifts and surprises tell him you care. Togetherness for you is being in a mutually sharing relationship where genuine concern for each other is foremost. Your ability to always show you care is sexy. Your thoughtfulness makes others feel safe and tells them in a very special way that they mean the world to you.

Keeping It Hot

You are personable, yet guarded. Keeping your distance protects your very sensitive side until you can discern what's best for you. When you know what you want, however, you don't hesitate. You go for it.

If you chose yellow as your least favorite primary color: You are devoted. Problems occur when you get carried away with supporting other people. You lose your ability to know what's best for you or your loved one. Your relationships can suffer. When you're upset, your warmth disappears. Don't say a word—lead with your heart. Your criticism can push the limits, and that will only make things worse.

If you chose blue as your least favorite primary color: Your dedication is unparalleled. Commitment, however, can be an issue—especially in dating. Your critical questions can miss the point or end communications entirely. Keep your warmth foremost. Speak from your heart and your love life will blossom.

How to Captivate a Red-Orange-Black

If your romantic partner loves red, orange, and black: Be up front. Understand that when your romantic partner tells you something, his mind is already made up. Expect it and don't get defensive. Agree with his point of view and then express yours. He's only close-minded at the beginning, especially if you touch on past disappointments. Later, he'll open up. When he pops your fantasy bubble, don't take it personally. Instead, listen. For better or for worse, honor your loved one's straight-from-the-heart comments. It will fuel his already strong sense of devotion to you, keep you both on track, and enable a more intimate connection. Together, you'll flourish—becoming closer and closer.

WORKPLACE

Your Key to Success

If you love red, orange, and black: Your focused ability to see what's not working is amazing. When things go off course, you're not afraid to express your opinion. You sail your own ship by constantly examining, in detail, what needs to be done. This is your great talent. Your agendas and goals are a crafted personal expression of you. Others expect you to get the ball rolling. Since you don't feel the need to conform, you see easier ways to get things done or the best ways to increase profitability.

Using facts compiled from past mistakes and successes, you deliver strong opinions that are hard to refute. Others learn invaluable information from your critiques about the efficiency of a project.

Investing in You

Your loyalty and commitment create a powerful bond with work colleagues. This is your key to success. Don't hesitate to point out if something is amiss. But reassure others that your penetrating gaze is all about helping them in the long run. Otherwise, they will see your perfectionist nature as threatening.

Jobs in which others can benefit from your support, such as computer repair, child care, or selling a product or service, are best for you. So look for situations where you can lend a hand. A word of caution: it's hard for you to discern what or who is contributing to your growth when you become too close. Back off. Distance will give you a new perspective.

How to Motivate a Red-Orange-Black

If your colleague loves red, orange, and black: Give your coworker the control to get things done. Then rest assured that this somewhat maverick red-orange-black will do only what's already been proved successful. Even when your colleague appears to have made up his mind, chances are the next day he will suggest a compromise. Keep the faith: he'll continue working toward a mutual agreement. In fact, your coworker's strong sense of devotion to you and the task at hand keeps him moving forward. Without it, he'll become spiritually bankrupt. He needs to feel needed and will even sacrifice his personal life for the good of the company.

RED, ORANGE, AND WHITE

ROMANCE

What's Sexy About You

If you love red, orange, and white: Your very personal yet somewhat unavailable appearance is sexy. In dating, no one has a clue as to how lovable you are. They mostly see your ability to set priorities and maximize each event into more fun. Your direct approach to the issues at hand gives you the ability to keep your relationships on track. By being aware of the underlying dynamics of your connection, you're able to create a sincere appreciation for the other person. What you find sexy is being in a very close relationship where both partners are not afraid to speak from the heart.

Keeping It Hot

You're a vivacious lover. Meeting new people is a turn-on. But don't become a victim of excess. In the end, your great need for intimacy will determine your happiness. Don't let feelings be turned into facts and vice versa. New doesn't always mean better. Focus on those who can give you love or your heart will become empty.

If you chose yellow as your least favorite primary color: You are on a journey to find an everlasting love, one that touches your heart and soul. Don't let your ability to forever create exciting situations get in the way. Slow down and others will see the genuine, lovable you. You simply need more time to feel close or even be understood by someone. Otherwise, you can lose sight of your own happiness.

If you chose blue as your least favorite primary color: Being with someone who completely loves you is vital. Total dedication to someone pulls your life together. But you can hide these feelings from others and sometimes even yourself. Others can react negatively to your unbiased comments, feeling that you don't care about them. Make the commitment to let your heart lead by showing your emotional side. Others will see that all your sincere concerns are your way of showing love.

How to Captivate a Red-Orange-White

If your romantic partner loves red, orange, and white: Always keep your red-orange-white at the top of your list. Loyalty turns him on. However, if your priorities slip, he will tell you in no uncertain terms. Your partner intuitively knows, right away, when your thoughts are not in his behalf. Dedication is what he needs. Anything less will send confusing messages and make it difficult for him to be close to you. Moreover, your significant other will become lost and start playing games—denying his own feelings. Don't let self-doubt cloud your great love. Just be you, and don't ever question your romantic partner's intentions. Know that his amazing sincerity will honor every facet of you, especially your vulnerabilities. An amazing great love, full of endearing affection, will be your treasure.

WORKPLACE

Your Key to Success

If you love red, orange, and white: Your ability to critique things without bias turns good ideas into great ones. But your strength goes even further. When you're allowed to contribute, you assemble problem-solving points of view, better utilize resources, and find easier ways to complete tasks. What others consider details or "small matters" you expand into better, more profitable ways to accomplish a task. This is your great talent. Use your eye-opening powers to connect resources and transform little ponds into big ones.

Investing in You

Choose work environments that give you the autonomy to show others better ways to use resources. This latitude increases your focus and productivity and allows those in charge to recognize exactly what you can accomplish. Their appreciation of your capabilities builds your self-confidence.

Consider running your own business or pursuing a career in child care, career counseling, patent law, or computer technology. A word of caution: don't let "the little things" keep you from achieving the big things. If you feel emotional, back off and refocus on your long-term goal.

How to Motivate a Red-Orange-White

If your colleague loves red, orange, and white: Follow your coworker's lead and you'll discover an entirely new world of usable resources and powerful perspectives that can create vast improvements. Difficult tasks will become easy, even fun. Pay attention to the details that he highlights—each one of them tells a story of how to fix something or redirect a program or a goal. Put one of your colleague's revelations to work. For example, turn his advice on an easier way to accomplish a task into a new company policy. Doing so will fuel not only his passions but also his respect for you. You will have found a true friend.

RED, ORANGE, AND BROWN

ROMANCE

What's Sexy About You

If you love red, orange, and brown: Your romantic partner gets easily attached to you. You're there to protect your significant other and make sure that he is honored and respected. When you fight for your loved one, you're fighting for yourself as well. Togetherness for you is a dedicated relationship, full of hugs, where you constantly identify what's not working and how to make things better. At times, however, your critique of situations going wrong overwhelms what's going right. Your partner can take it personally, get defensive, and end up with a wounded ego. Give him more time to discover his mistakes by asking questions, not solving issues.

Keeping It Hot

To understand the more intimate you, select another achromatic color. Do you prefer black or white? After you've selected your preference, turn to the appropriate page to read your personalized love tips.

If you prefer black, you're a red-orange-black (see page 112). If you prefer white, you're a red-orange-white (see page 115).

WORKPLACE

Your Key to Success

If you love red, orange, and brown: Nothing escapes your sharp gaze. Your direct approach to every task eliminates misconceptions. In being more concerned about what's actually occurring around you rather than in people's interpretations, you assemble all the pertinent facts. This is your great talent. Your forte is inspecting supportive devices or the quality of products or services. At your best, your concerns have healing power. Express yourself by giving others physical assistance or emotional reassurance. You'll strengthen your own spirit in the process.

Investing in You

Use your awareness of things and events to fix problems and pull things together. You're going to be an amazing detective, whatever you do, so find an occupation in which you can express your rare talent.

Consider careers in operations, quality assurance, manufacturing, product development, forensic science, or any field where your critical, sharp eye can identify problems or things that aren't working. A word of caution: at times your critical nature can overshadow the people you care about the most or hinder the completion of a task that is vital to your success. When you feel emotional, slow down and think of a diplomatic, tactful way to get your point across or you will turn off those around you.

How to Motivate a Red-Orange-Brown

If your colleague loves red, orange, and brown: This inspector's eagle eye sees how to correct things efficiently. Don't fight it. After all, his process-oriented awareness is unparalleled. Just celebrate your coworker's ability to keep things moving. Even when his tone sounds critical, rise above it. It's simply not about you. It's his knee-jerk response to constant challenges. Honor your colleague for his dedication to you and the task at hand. Then be prepared for an entirely new person to arrive on the scene, one motivated to give back unrelenting support. Honesty is all a red-orange-brown expects.

PART THREE

COMBINATIONS

What Your Colors Say About Your Relationship

CHAPTER THIRTEEN

Primary Connection

Your Basic Motivators

The great thing in life is not so much where we stand, as in what direction we are moving.

—OLIVER WENDELL HOLMES

The primary colors—yellow, blue, and red—indicate the main sources of your energy. Knowing your friend's, family member's, romantic partner's, or coworker's primary color connections will give you both the power to realize what drives you. Fire up your engines! Experience together how your color choices merge to keep your life goals on track. Review your primary color ranking on pages 16–17 before you begin.

In this first of four interactive chapters, you should concentrate on understanding your one-of-a-kind interpersonal chemistry. Enjoy how you and your partner mix and match to support, charm, and motivate each other. Reading about each other's core motivation will enable both of you to better tap into your own passions and gain the strength to look past distracting incidental details.

Finally, once you learn the best ways to support each other's core life motivation, you can take the ultimate power step and turn each other's untapped energy into positive actions. Your life together will become more enjoyable, meaningful, and successful.

YOUR FIRST-CHOICE PRIMARY CHEMISTRY

In this section, you'll learn how to set and gauge goals with friends, family, romantic partners, and coworkers. Determining your core passion connection will empower you to craft a more cohesive, respectful, and productive future together.

If Your First Choice Matches Their First Choice

If you and your partner share the same primary color, you can more easily understand each other's core being. His or her goals are very much like yours.

YELLOW 1ST MEETS YELLOW 1ST

Key Words: Realistic, Diplomatic, Giving

Yellow Motivation: To learn and personally grow

Together: You see each other's points of view

The two of you are always talking! You spend time in constant conversation about the pleasant things in life. Your relationship is like a melody. You both effortlessly attract into your circle of friends others who provide new sources of stimulation. When the two of you disagree, you simply change the subject. However, don't avoid confrontation too often: this evasion will weaken your relationship.

Family and Friends: Supportive Tips

The two of you become so immersed in what you're doing that others may say you live in your own world. And there's never a dull moment: even an ordinary errand like going to the supermarket can turn into an adventure. Appreciate the many ways you support each other and exchange advice. Use your natural bond to keep your strength, even when you're being invaded by rules-oriented reds or agenda-ridden blues. Everyone benefits from your ability to show the real meaning of friendship and family.

Romance and Dating: Love Tips

Love between you two is a charming excursion. You just can't believe that you're romantically involved with such a genuine, down-to-earth person. Protect your bond by not getting carried away with your need to help other family members or friends. For example, avoid answering all of Mom's phone calls, constantly bailing out friends, or giving the children all your attention. Keep things exciting by reminding yourself and your partner every day that you are with the love of your life.

Workplace: Team-Building Tips

When working together, two yellows are a duo who takes into account everyone else's point of view—a very powerful tool in the workplace. You contemplate endless ways to approach every task and envision what needs to be done. Be careful: you may miss the point altogether or get sidetracked if there are too many possible solutions on the table. Still, you know it's important to keep a discussion open until all the angles have been properly considered. Otherwise, a red's bossy side or a blue's close-mindedness can disrupt your back-and-forth flow of information, and you won't be able to complete the task at hand in the most efficient way.

BLUE 1ST MEETS BLUE 1ST

Key Words: Planner, Initiator, Visionary

Blue Motivation: To picture how things fit together

Together: You encourage each other to seek your dreams

The two of you stay focused on the future. You talk about your plans. You see your partner's wishes as if they were a reality. You encourage each another to "just do it"—to quickly complete each task and move on to the next. When you disagree, there is little to talk about at first. You both believe you are right. However, after your initial clash you usually compromise, since neither of you is comfortable with interpersonal conflict.

Family and Friends: Supportive Tips

You confirm each other's dreams. Visions of receiving applause or fame and fortune for a job well done fire up your conversations. Without the intrusion of practicality, you can laugh and have fun talking about ideas, even if you have no desire to follow through on them. As a blue duo, you should learn to appreciate reds for their no-holds-barred advice, even though they disrupt your calming mood, and yellows for their grounding concerns, even though they're all too ready to bring you back to reality.

Romance and Dating: Love Tips

Together you create an idealistic world. Learn to honor your disagreements by actually discussing them instead of hoping that they'll go away. Otherwise, unrealistic expectations will constantly rain on your lovely parade. Embrace your differences with a calm demeanor, even when you have strong opposing opinions. Give each other the space you need to be yourselves.

Workplace: Team-Building Tips

The two of you stay focused on your ambitions. Your mutual admiration for each other's contributions is the key to your own self-confidence. When you agree, you're an inspiration to your coworkers. But be careful: if your blue partner upsets your vision, you'll lose it. If this happens, simply understand that each of you has a different picture in his or her head that will probably achieve the same end result. Take the time to openly discuss your thoughts: you'll soon find a new solution that both of you can get behind.

RED 1ST MEETS RED 1ST

Key Words: Curious, Resourceful, Direct

Red Motivation: To better control your world

Together: You create practical solutions

Some may call you gossip mavens, but you're both genuinely concerned about those close to you. Marriages, dates, divorces, and sibling rivalries are big topics, and no detail is too small to pique your interest. Both of you enjoy discussing how others are living their lives, as they open up new perspectives on how to best live your own. But beware: if one of you dwells on a dilemma, the other will take over and become bossy. Disagreement ensues.

Family and Friends: Supportive Tips

The two of you love to get together with friends and talk about how everyone else is doing. To improve your energy, avoid mean gossip. Instead, express sincere concerns, without adding all the juicy stuff you've heard. Try to stick to the facts—don't speculate! The direct way that you both speak to each other won't work with other family members. Honor them by backing off and crafting a more diplomatic approach. Then express what needs to be said, but don't make it sound like you're giving an order.

Romance and Dating: Love Tips

Your romance is a passionate, physical adventure with shared responsibilities. Knowing what you are going to do and what your partner will do makes you feel secure. You both run your day with a predetermined set of rules. This is a turn-on, but it can backfire: if you cross over your partner's personal boundary, there'll be hell to pay. Fights can erupt over issues that later seem of little importance. Constantly pamper your partner and don't allow indifference to dispel your desires.

Workplace: Team-Building Tips

Two reds evaluate projects and the people around them with a practical eye. You're both genuinely concerned about coworkers close to you and look out for their best interests. Your analytical minds feed on detail and you believe strongly in doing each project right the first time. Your strong critiques and need to do things a certain way can be destructive, however. Adapt rules to fit everyone's natural style, not just yours.

Your First Choice Mixes with Their First Choice

If you and your partner choose different primary colors, each of you will find a different way to accomplish the same goal. In this section, you'll learn how to benefit the most from your partner's leadership style.

YELLOW 1ST MEETS BLUE 1ST

Key Words: Realistic, Diplomatic, Giving meets

Planner, Initiator, Visionary

Yellow Motivation: To learn and personally grow

Blue Motivation: To picture how things fit together

Together: You constantly discuss how to best get things done

As a yellow, you teach your blue how to enjoy each day and appreciate different perspectives. Your considerations demonstrate the art of flexibility. Your blue gains the power to be more open, see new resources, and acquire realistic expectations. You make him feel more like a winner. In a crisis, you know when your blue is losing his grip on reality—becoming consumed by expectations.

As a blue, you help your yellow clarify future goals. You turn her factual perspective into a plan. You admire your yellow's flexibility, yet become frustrated when you feel that goals are not being met. You may even see your yellow as being indecisive or lacking direction.

Family and Friends: Supportive Tips

As a yellow, make your blue a winner by getting him to slow down. He'll become grounded, envision what he needs to do, and be more in touch with others' points of view, especially yours. He'll become a lot more considerate, too.

As a blue, keep your yellow on track by constantly reminding her of all the important things that she's doing. Sincere appreciation will fuel her self-confidence. As a blue-yellow duo, you can make your life together more relaxed.

Romance and Dating: Love Tips

A yellow's giving, considerate nature allows a blue partner to be himself. Open up his life by getting him to break his routine, live more in the moment, or consider more comfortable ways for you both to live as a couple. Make his house feel more like a home.

A blue's romantic notions keep things exciting. Your obvious vulnerability is sexy to your yellow. Keeping you grounded makes her feel needed. You create a supportive home together.

Workplace: Team-Building Tips

As a yellow, get your blue to consider all available information before making a decision. Don't take him seriously when it appears that he's completely made up his mind. He's still open to your suggestions and truly needs your advice. Teach him profitable new ways to solve a problem or get someone to hear what he is saying.

As a blue, keep your yellow focused by creating a final product vision or listing specific goals for her to accomplish. Don't fence her in with unnecessary boundaries, exact ways to do something, or hard rules. You both get the job profitably done and ensure, along the way, that you've made the right choices together.

BLUE 1ST MEETS RED 1ST

Key Words: Planner, Initiator, Visionary meets

Curious, Resourceful, Direct

Blue Motivation: To picture how things fit together

Red Motivation: To better control your world

Together: You do it right the first time

As a blue, you never fail to entertain a red with your ideas. You encourage the more task-oriented red to dream and grasp a larger vision. You make looking forward to the future more fun. In a crisis, your ego may become wounded, causing you to discount your red's contributions and dismiss his input as negative and nonconstructive.

As a red, you coach your blue on how to pinpoint specific actions to accomplish her ideas. You force her to face limitations. With your chop, chop, chop, you cut out what's not necessary to make ideas work. When your blue ignores your input, you discount her creative contributions. You see her as being unaware of vital details.

Family and Friends: Supportive Tips

As a blue, you feel that reds are just too bossy. Don't label them or call them names; instead of ignoring their advice, benefit from their decisive nature. Protecting you is the goal of your red friend or family member. Rebellion or indifference will only make things worse. If you're the parent of a red child, ask him for advice on how to get things done. He'll take charge and make your life together a joy.

Being too direct as a red will make it hard for a blue to hear you. If you feel emotional, back off. Your advice should be stern but calm. Back up every order with a neutral, nonaccusatory question that forces your blue to fully digest the consequences of how she would feel or what would occur if she followed your instructions.

Romance and Dating: Love Tips

As a blue, simply accept that your red's rules have your best interest in mind. Don't take it personally when his protective advice seems to undermine your best ideas or his bossy side wounds your ego. Being confrontational will get you nowhere.

Your blue shows her love for you through what she says. Later on, propose a different way. She'll be more receptive.

A red's directness is sexy. Being your physical, expressive self will stir your blue's imagination and her romantic side as well. To maintain peace around the house, prod your blue to pinpoint the specific actions needed to turn an idea into a reality. Even if you know all the answers, prompt your blue to discover them on her own by asking her questions.

Workplace: Team-Building Tips

A blue needs a red's input to be successful. Don't create an implementation plan for your goals without your red: it's a waste of time. Lighten up—make the discussion a game. Simply present your plans to him and ask what could go wrong. Take notes. He will appreciate your trust. Then get back to him on each point.

As a red, you'll be better able to give sound advice if you challenge your blue to write her plans down: "Sounds great, but how can we do it and what will it cost?" In the process, she discovers on her own the sequence, resources, and details required for success. And as a team, you discover winning solutions.

RED 1ST MEETS YELLOW 1ST

Key Words: Curious, Resourceful, Direct meets

Realistic, Diplomatic, Giving

Red Motivation: To better control your world

Yellow Motivation: To learn and personally grow

Together: You create better ways to live

As a red, you teach your yellow how to target performance by being more specific. Your yellow loves your knowledgeable ways, but too many rules can make him feel confined and unable to function. In a crisis, you may become upset with your yellow for not confronting personal issues or current dilemmas.

As a yellow, you allow your red to see the limitations of her rules and agendas. You help her become more flexible— better able to enjoy possessions and friendships. With your support, your red feels less confined and more able to relax. But don't stop there. Use your diplomatic skills to teach your red to consider others' points of view before she speaks. Your red-yellow connection builds a fun, productive, and practical relationship.

Family and Friends: Supportive Tips

As a red, you set firm rules to protect your family from harm. But your yellow needs to hear the rationale behind your demands. So, instead of barking an order, loosen up and try a considerate request. You'll gain the affection and love that you deserve in return.

As a yellow, you give grounded advice that keeps your family together. Don't let your red's bossy side intimidate you. Appeal to her softer side with kindness and appreciation for what she's done. Together, you'll create a very fun friendship or family that will have the strength to withstand any crisis.

Romance and Dating: Love Tips

The physicality and forward demeanor of a red are sexy. Your heartfelt protective advice and concerns about how your yellow feels constantly remind him of how much you care. Turn on your yellow by being more open. Try to see both points of view in a conversation, instead of making a fast judgment or offering a curt opinion. Your yellow won't think of you as pushy, and your needs will become his focus.

A yellow's open-minded persona is sexy, even magnetic,

to a red. Protect yourself by remembering that your red's inflexible routines and schedules are all about her, not you. Counsel your red to be less judgmental and more appreciative of everyone's point of view. This advice makes your life together more intimate. Sweep your red off her feet!

Workplace: Team-Building Tips

As a red, protect the bottom line by ensuring that a project's proposed risks are no different from what's been successfully undertaken in the past. Then put your yellow's ability to see others' points of view to good use. Ask him how to best approach new situations or make a vivid presentation.

As a yellow, make sure your red has considered every side of the story before making a decision. Capture her attention by suggesting that she reconsider old ideas or unexpected resources. Together, you solve workplace dilemmas, enlist team support, and use resources for their ultimate purpose.

YOUR SECOND-CHOICE PRIMARY CHEMISTRY

As you read about your second primary color choice below, take pride in how the perspectives of both you and your partner bring out each other's softer side. You center yourself and your family and friends in these colors.

Your Second Choice Calms Their First Choice

Your second primary choice naturally calms the excessive passions of your partner's first choice. Just by being yourself, you create a quieting effect that infuses a more balanced, supportive point of view.

YELLOW 2ND MEETS YELLOW 1ST

As a second-choice yellow, you effortlessly make your first-choice yellow more decisive. You highlight but don't push vital issues that need to be addressed, which allows your first-choice yellow to be less bogged down in the details of a situation and more focused on the future result. When the two of you are together, you recognize all the elements needed for success.

As a first-choice yellow, you need a flexible environment where you can investigate all the facts before arriving at an answer. Solutions unfold when you are partnered with a second-choice yellow. If you become overwhelmed, she lets you know in no uncertain terms that you're ignoring your own needs.

BLUE 2ND MEETS BLUE 1ST

As a second-choice blue, you allow a first-choice blue to see different ways of deciphering situations. Visualizing a variety of achievable methods keeps him from being overwhelmed by his ideas. When you spend one-on-one time with a first-choice blue, you turn his headstrong comments into workable plans.

As a first-choice blue, you are a passionate, imaginative dreamer who loves to create original ideas. Your preoccupation with the future gives a second-choice blue the mental discipline to not only stay on track but also encourage others to do the same. When you are overwhelmed, however, your preoccupation with your own ideas can make you unrealistic. But when paired with a second-choice blue, you can together realize your dreams for the future.

RED 2ND MEETS RED 1ST

As a second-choice red, you temper your first-choice red's rules-oriented world. Breathe life into his judgment calls by reminding him to refrain from constantly evaluating situations and others' performance. As a result, he will more carefully consider the advantages as well as the consequences of his actions.

As a passionate first-choice red, you are direct, driven, outgoing, and know exactly what you want. Your firm rules create workable plans. However, when you are overwhelmed, you enforce them too rigidly. When you spend one-on-one time with your second-choice red, you loosen up and envision not only how to get the job done but also how to keep everyone else engaged.

Your Second Choice Uplifts Their Third Choice

Your second-choice primary selection provides a pillar of strength for the third-choice primary selection of your friend, family member, romantic partner, or coworker. Your interaction channels frustrations into positive actions and, in an emotional crisis, imparts powerful self-truths to your third-choice friend.

YELLOW 2ND MEETS YELLOW 3RD

Just by being yourself, as a second-choice yellow, you create a calming presence for your third-choice yellow. When his sense of urgency requires an answer—sometimes even before he knows the facts—you slow him down. You remind him to work at a more reasonable pace. With a renewed, more realistic perspective, he gets things done right the first time.

As an emotional third-choice yellow, you are focused and headstrong. Your "right now" attitude gets the job done, but you can be rude. Without taking things personally, your second-choice yellow encourages you to loosen up, make apologies, and proceed on a more realistic track.

BLUE 2ND MEETS BLUE 3RD

As a second-choice blue, you have realistic goals and formulate achievable plans. You rescue your third-choice blue from myriad little tasks that seem to overwhelm his long-term goals. In return, learn from his ability to critique without bias everything and everyone around him.

As a third-choice blue, you see different ways to decipher situations. You're great at categorizing what's most helpful, setting standards, and judging people's performance. When you become entangled in your own agendas, however, you can win the battle and lose the war. Don't lose sight of the future. You can constantly improve the quality of your lives together, as long as one keeps the other on track.

RED 2ND MEETS RED 3RD

As a second-choice red, you encourage your timid third-choice red to talk about how he feels. By not pushing for immediate answers, you give him more time to express himself. Since the third choice thoroughly considers each situation, you also gain valuable, in-depth information.

As a third-choice red, you analyze your thoughts before you speak. This pause enables you to articulate your feelings and concerns, encompassing all points of view. Not revealing your thoughts up front, however, can make your life harder to manage. As partners, don't rush; you both need to allow for points of view to resonate, before you decide how to make positive improvements in your lives.

YOUR THIRD-CHOICE PRIMARY CHEMISTRY

Your third-choice connection highlights issues that you usually avoid discussing with friends and coworkers. Embrace the powerful concerns of your emotions with heartfelt understanding. If you don't, you risk fomenting excessive or impulsive situations, especially if you try to label feelings as "right" or "wrong."

Your Third Choice Meets Their First Choice

An overall view on the first choice can be a pillar of strength for the third choice. In a crisis, however, a clash between the two can upset the status quo. Frustrations heighten sensitivity, and positive actions stall.

YELLOW 3RD MEETS YELLOW 1ST

As a third-choice yellow, when you feel upset, your sense of urgency can make your first-choice yellow upset. You want him to be more decisive, to say or know exactly what he is going to do.

As a first-choice yellow, you make your third-choice yellow aware of each moment and better able to enjoy life's daily pleasures. Your concern and ability to see her point of view teaches her how to make swift decisions.

Family and Friends: Supportive Tips

As a third-choice yellow, you need to be patient. When you pressure your first-choice-yellow family member or friend, not only will he refuse to hear what you say, but he will disappear for a while. Keep him on track by asking questions, but don't badger him. Give him time to consider his options thoroughly, or you'll lose his support.

When your third-choice yellow is in a rush, she can be a demanding jerk. As a first-choice yellow, you shouldn't take it personally. Instead, simply stop everything and ask for a hug or change the subject. Bring it up with her again later, and things will be just fine.

Workplace: Team-Building Tips

As a third-choice yellow, you should never start anything until you ask a first-choice yellow for his opinion. His way of getting that first appointment with a difficult prospective client or merely getting you or others to hear the full extent of what you're proposing is beyond compare. Benefit from the powerful perspectives of your first-choice yellow.

As a first-choice yellow, team up with a third-choice yellow when multiple considerations make a decision overwhelming. Your knowledgeable concerns and her goal-focused thoughts create on-target decisions.

BLUE 3RD MEETS BLUE 1ST

As a third-choice blue, you are often appalled by your first-choice blue's unrealistic expectations: why does he always assume the best-case scenario? By reviewing each issue or situation critically, you draft a list of must-do tasks. Your observations set higher standards for him.

Your exciting, cohesive vision of what lies ahead as a first-choice blue pulls together your third-choice blue's life. However, your ideas can miss vital criteria that diminish your effectiveness. But you can create the functional plans that you cannot devise by yourself with the help of your third-choice blue.

Family and Friends: Supportive Tips

As a third-choice blue, encourage your first-choice blue to discuss his strategy with you about what he's going to do. Then repeat back to him what he's told you, until he learns how to best deal with issues. Otherwise, he will transform your concerned questions into disapproval, and conclude that he doesn't measure up.

As a first-choice blue, advise your third-choice blue to envision pictures of the journey ahead. Her haphazard to-do list coalesces into a step-by-step plan that is more workable. Together you learn smoother ways to grow and move forward in your lives.

Workplace: Team-Building Tips

As a third-choice blue, you teach your first-choice blue that greatness is in the details. With your never-ending concerns about quality, you hold projects, events, or presentations to a higher standard. Projects and events are a rousing success. You may become consumed by the volume of details, however, and miss the point.

As a first-choice blue, don't frown on your third-choice blue's occasionally harsh comments. Just because she disagrees with you doesn't mean that she's not a team player. Even if your third-choice blue is wrong, chances are there's a vital perspective behind her message. You can create amazing things together that raise the bar of excellence to its highest level.

RED 3RD MEETS RED 1ST

As a third-choice red, you encourage your first-choice red to shrug off the small stuff. At first you appreciate how your first-choice red protects you and encourages you to stand up for yourself. But later you may view his telling you what to do as "bossy" and feel resentful.

As a first-choice red, you have heartfelt concerns that keep your third-choice red on track. Your rules about her expressing what's needed ensure that she's respected by everyone around her. Together you learn how being respectful in a relationship creates a very fluid, supportive bond.

Family and Friends: Supportive Tips

As a third-choice red, you get upset when your first-choice red barks orders. Even if he has the solution, it doesn't matter—you rebel. You need more time to analyze considerations. Demand it when your first-choice red becomes pushy. He will understand. Otherwise, you will lose yourself. If you are a third-choice-red parent, be more specific about what you expect from your child. She will feel safer.

As a first-choice-red parent or friend, you make your third-choice feel safe. Ask her to confront recurring unpleasant issues. Tell her to prioritize what's most important. Her profound answers will surprise you. Challenge your third-choice red by asking more questions instead of giving instructions. Get her to be more specific and to write her ideas down.

Workplace: Team-Building Tips

A third-choice red's natural curiosity reveals facts that expose invaluable information. When confronted with a question, don't give an immediate yes or no answer. Tell your first-choice red that you need to give the issue some thought and you will get back to him later with the specifics.

As a first-choice red, you deliver very specific instructions. Get your third-choice red to do the same by encouraging her to write down her ideas. This routine will force her to create a specific action plan. Ask your third-choice red tough questions, but don't expect an answer right away. Her thought process takes longer, but her thoroughness keeps others from dropping the ball.

Your Third Choice Meets Their Third Choice

Discover together your shared primary obstacle to success. Your unfulfilled concerns, those issues and experiences that you usually avoid, can be bonding experiences. In a crisis, however, one of you will have to step outside of your comfort zone to get your relationship back on track.

YELLOW 3RD MEETS YELLOW 3RD

You are both exceptionally goal oriented and clearly grasp the objective at hand. You admire each other's determination and focus. If one of you is in a hurry, however, your "now or never" exaggerated sense of urgency can make you appear very selfish. A crisis will erupt. An apology will then be expected later on, or you'll have to redo something.

Relationship Tips

Keep it fun! When the other one feels that an issue or position is impossible, don't be so stubborn. Back away. Dispel your expectations—especially if one of you feels emotional about it. Calm down. Then set up new, more realistic plans. And this time, don't rush. You'll be more successful, and the day's simple pleasures will make your relationship and life hum.

BLUE 3RD MEETS BLUE 3RD

The two of you see different ways to decipher situations. Since you are both fair critics, you are naturals at setting standards and judging people's performance. You both know how to categorize what's most helpful. Be on guard. Committing to your future plans, or even to each other, may be exhausting. When one of you is upset, things become boring. Conversations go in circles.

Relationship Tips

Loosen up! Stay focused on your main objective and don't get distracted by excessive concerns. Wake up to a bigger picture that presents more global results. Then take a risk. Just do it. Otherwise, both of you will find it hard to get beyond your own agendas. Everything will feel like a task.

RED 3RD MEETS RED 3RD

You truly appreciate each other's thoughtful, deferential manner. Together you create an atmosphere that reinforces what you both like about yourselves. At times, however, you may feel uncomfortable with each other. You both prefer people who say what's on their mind. It drives you crazy when you suspect that your partner is withholding information.

Relationship Tips

Keep it fun! Express what you're thinking, and encourage your partner to do the same. Be very specific. Don't talk around issues. Take notes when necessary and follow up. Writing things down now gives you the power to reevaluate your situation later. Even though this process is time-consuming, it enables you and your partner to support each other, stay more organized, and feel closer, especially in a crisis.

CHAPTER FOURTEEN

Secondary Connection

How You Relate

People are lonely because they build walls instead of bridges.
—Joseph F. Newton

Green, purple, and orange reflect your thinking process and indicate how you relate to people. It is through your secondary color connections with your friends, family, romantic partners, and coworkers that you experience others' most considerate thoughts. Review your secondary color ranking on page 16 before you begin.

These interactive pages will strengthen your relationships. Both of you will gain an understanding of each other's needs, choices, and contributions. Reading this together will give you the knowledge to honor each other's heartfelt thoughtfulness as a great gift.

Enjoy how your secondary color choices connect. Look beyond superficial disagreements that distract you from being open and learn how to turn emotions into supportive actions. Use this system to form a shared, renewed bond that enriches your daily conversations.

YOUR FIRST-CHOICE SECONDARY CHEMISTRY

These colors reflect how you reason with your friends, family, romantic partners, and coworkers. They reveal your foremost concerns about how to best achieve your desires, fulfill your needs, and realize your goals.

Your 1st Choice Matches Their 1st Choice

If you and your partner share the same secondary color, each of you understands how the other thinks. As you read, reflect on the powerful, soothing benefits (and occasionally frustrating consequences!) of your shared thought connections.

GREEN 1ST MEETS GREEN 1ST

Key Words: Nurturing, Concerned, Comfortable

Green Power: Creating supportive environments

Together: You know how to best help each other

Both of you admire the way the other takes the time to stop and listen. At your best, you give each other a stronger sense of self. When you offer supportive advice, you both feel good about yourselves, which, in turn, creates a positive aura for those around you. Your relationship is an emotionally safe haven where you both can take refuge to better understand yourselves. Of course, you read each other so well that at your worst you see the other's selfish thoughts.

Family and Friends: Supportive Tips

The green-green parent-child bond and friendship connections are so close that many times you feel like mirror images. Use your psychic connection to encourage each other when times get tough. If you find fault with your other green's irritating habits, look again. This time dig a little deeper—you will see a bit of yourself. Your genuine concern for each other makes your house a home.

Romance and Dating: Love Tips

When first meeting, each green admires the other's kindness and intellect. As romantic partners, you are both at ease, knowing that the other's life goals are also yours. You both seek a loving home, and this is especially beneficial when you have a child. Don't take each other for granted. If you let things get too comfortable, your romantic flame will flicker.

Workplace: Team-Building Tips

Green duos constantly discuss how to achieve goals. By listening with concern, each partner encourages the other to find solutions. You increase profitability by anticipating potential roadblocks. Use your tuned-in, nonthreatening approach to make others more aware of possible obstacles. Teach people skills to your colleagues—for example, instruct them on how to be more responsive to a client's request.

PURPLE 1ST MEETS PURPLE 1ST

Key Words: Dramatic, Determined, Empowering

Purple Power: Seeing possibilities, ideas, and strategies

Together: You make the impossible possible

The two of you see possibilities in everything. You're the first to embrace novel ideas and create new things, from starting a fashion trend to inventing a recipe. Your wit and sense of drama add a playful quality and excitement to your lives. Others may believe the two of you are arguing, when in fact intellectual sparring is just your way of having fun. At your worst, you have a tendency to dramatize "facts," thereby obscuring the truth. In a crisis, your assumptions may make you pessimistic or paranoid.

Family and Friends: Supportive Tips

Your strong purple-purple psychic connection allows you to speak to each other without words. Knowing the other's thoughts before you speak helps to reinforce your self-image and challenges both of you to become more determined—to fight for your dreams. Keep family members on track by suggesting strategies to get ahead. Avoid envious thoughts, and you'll have all you need.

Romance and Dating: Love Tips

Your déjà-vu romance is magical. Do you remember when you first met? It was as if you'd already known each other for years. You and your partner relate to everyone else in the same way—you're both determined to unmask others' true motivations. However, frustrations brew when your different expectations about the relationship clash. Discuss each partner's life dreams before setting your heart on making them a reality. If you keep your expectations grounded, your journey together will become an even more exciting adventure.

Workplace: Team-Building Tips

Both purples are natural leaders in the world of business—talented at formulating successful strategies and motivating others. But trouble can loom when you too quickly agree with each other! Both of you may assume erroneously that you already know how to do something when in fact you don't. Ask more questions: What does my client need? Has my coworker completed his project? Check out every vital consideration thoroughly or you will waste time and money.

ORANGE 1ST MEETS ORANGE 1ST

Key Words: Bold, Dedicated, Sentimental

Orange Power: Implementing change without disruption

Together: You enjoy life's simple pleasures

The two of you are fun, warm, and lovable. Each encourages the other to express a bold social persona. At your best, you readily acknowledge each other's contributions, daily accomplishments, and successes. People see you both as sentimental one moment and strictly logical the next. At your worst, both of you are hypercritical and petty, constantly pointing out minor transgressions.

Family and Friends: Supportive Tips

Go ahead, play a video game or attend a sporting event or concert. Doing things together will not only get your relationship back on track but also, ironically, give you the confidence to experiment more on your own. Tell family members how much you enjoy their company. You laugh with friends about their life-in-the-fast-lane side, but secretly plot to do anything to keep them safe!

Romance and Dating: Love Tips

Relish how your sensitive nature understands your partner's feelings without words. Your powerful emotional connection not only reinforces your day-to-day routines but also creates one sexy encounter after another. Keep your relationship humming by constantly planning fun dates and honoring your loved one's accomplishments.

Workplace: Team-Building Tips

You love to pick apart complicated issues together. You relish a challenge, but use your analytical side to create realistic work expectations and the means to accomplish them. Your combined energy gets things done in the most profitable way. Your fact-oriented questions ground each other, but be careful not to push too hard. You will start a turf war and find fault even with suggestions that work.

Your First Choice Mixes with Their First Choice

If you and your partner choose different secondary colors, it means each of you has an entirely different thinking style. Your partner's considerations will complement yours. As you read, contemplate both the beneficial concerns and the misinterpreted signals that each of you receives from the other.

GREEN 1ST MEETS PURPLE 1ST

Key Words: Nurturing, Concerned, Comfortable meets

Dramatic, Determined, Empowering

Green Power: Creating supportive environments

Purple Power: Seeing possibilities, ideas, and strategies

Together: You entertain and cherish each other

As a green, you show your purple how to slow down and enjoy the everyday pleasures of life. Your sincerity helps your purple feel comfortable with himself. He becomes more self-aware, better able to understand what he needs. In a personal crisis, however, your considerate nature retreats inward. Your purple can feel left out or even view you as self-absorbed.

As a purple, you help your green recognize empowering possibilities and become more self-confident. Your wit stimulates and encourages her to see the potential within. In a personal crisis, your green can feel that your questions are intrusive. But on the whole, your connection is very exciting.

Family and Friends: Supportive Tips

As a green, use your calming listening skills and sympathetic manner to bring your high-strung purple back to earth. Just being with you makes your purple comfortable with himself and creates a feeling of home.

As a purple, consider how to transform your kindhearted green into more of a tiger. Don't let her become too complacent, or she'll get stuck. If you see that she's unhappy with her romantic relationship or her job, question why she's staying. Encourage her to make a change. Yours is an empowering relationship built on each other's fundamental needs.

Romance and Dating: Love Tips

As a green, take charge of a situation by keeping things real. Keep your purple grounded by asking provocative questions. He'll find this sexy. And don't let the fact that you don't share hobbies or outlooks on life break the two of you apart—your differences keep your relationship spicy.

As a purple, keep things exciting on a mental level. Teach your green a new word a day, or offer up an interesting piece of trivia. Just be your entertaining self: your green will bask in a constant flood of adventures and stories.

Workplace: Team-Building Tips

As a green, use your ability to remain calm and collected under stress to anchor your excitable purple. Slow things down long enough to discern which strategies work best. If he is being overemotional, stop everything and get the facts. Trying to force something to happen will only end in disaster.

As a purple, keep your attention focused until the problem is solved. Challenge your green to consider new ideas or easier ways to get the job done. Pay attention to everything the green says, especially items that upset your plans. Consider all the facts and strategize a solution together.

PURPLE 1ST MEETS ORANGE 1ST

Key Words: Dramatic, Determined, Empowering meets

Bold, Dedicated, Sentimental

Purple Power: Seeing possibilities, ideas, and strategies

Orange Power: Implementing change without disruption

Together: You create a fun, successful future

Drama follows a purple around. But this isn't all bad—often it sparks positive change in your life, or at least a learning situation. Your orange is energized by your witty, clever thoughts. However, when you become distracted by grandiose ideas, he can't hear you. At that point, you may view your orange's grounding questions in a negative light.

An orange's analytical side encourages a purple to have more realistic expectations. Your fact-oriented questions reduce frustrations and make your purple feel secure. But don't be too consumed by the needs of others. Your purple can feel as though he's not being heard. The two of you create obtainable dreams together.

Family and Friends: Supportive Tips

As a purple, consider how your kind orange needs to change in order to live a more powerful life. Challenge his analytical thoughts without offending his sensitive side. Avoid off-the-wall or out-of-the-box strategies. But keep things honest. Otherwise, he will discount your advice.

As an orange, encourage your purple to ditch unreasonable expectations. Challenge her by crafting questions (something you do well) to formulate a plan that can be accomplished. Otherwise, constant frustrations will make her unhappy. Create a never-ending learning adventure together.

Romance and Dating: Love Tips

As a purple, don't expect your orange to see the same potential in himself that you see. Expand on all the things that he accomplishes by noting his contributions. In return, he will open his soft, teddy-bear side to you.

As an orange, don't let your purple's drama make you inattentive. A simple hug and an "I love you" will calm her mood and get her back on track.

Workplace: Team-Building Tips

As a purple, you energize your orange, helping to create exciting career possibilities for him. However, when you are distracted by grandiose ideas, your orange tunes you out. He views you as unrealistic—headed toward failure.

An orange's ability to ask the right questions makes your purple's clever strategies work. In a crisis, your purple may view you as too negative—finding fault with even good suggestions. Together the two of you create achievable work goals.

ORANGE 1ST MEETS GREEN 1ST

Key Words: Bold, Dedicated, Sentimental meets

Nurturing, Concerned, Comfortable

Orange Power: Implementing change without disruption

Green Power: Creating supportive environments

Together: You make each other feel important

As an orange, you give your green a positive, strong awareness of what he has accomplished. When a green feels proud, he becomes more self-confident and in control. In a personal crisis, however, you may view his critical comments as insensitive.

As a green, you reinvigorate an orange. You make the leap from passing thoughts to more relevant issues. You see the real, very sensitive orange. Your concerns allow her to be less defensive and better able to make genuine contributions. The two of you engender an open and inviting atmosphere.

Family and Friends: Supportive Tips

As an orange, protect your green from outsiders who take advantage of his goodness. Get him to create expectations that are more reasonable. Be your bold self by crafting questions—for example, What are you getting from this project?—that challenge your green to think. He will be happier and less frustrated.

As a green, use your supportive tips to get your orange to focus more on what she needs rather than belabor what's been done. Don't let your sensitive loved one get too sentimental or defensive. Your love of being at home together creates a powerful bond.

Romance and Dating: Love Tips

As an orange, don't hide the sensitive you. Your lovable, sentimental side makes you sexy—greens especially are turned on by it. Don't get so carried away with supporting others that your green feels forgotten. Concentrate your focus more on your romantic partner than your friends and he will instill an old-fashioned sense of home.

As a green, don't be shy when it comes to expressing your

knowledge. Your orange thinks smart partners are sexy. Use your supportive skills to create a world where your dedicated loved one can unwind. Your orange will, in turn, become a lovable teddy bear.

Workplace: Team-Building Tips

An orange's strong project-oriented persona energizes a green. Your support allows your green to be more self-confident and better able to tackle technical and operational details in a more thorough manner. Remember to start each discussion with what your green has done right. Otherwise, he will find it difficult to acknowledge what went wrong.

As a green, you reinvigorate an orange. By turning her analytical thoughts into more relevant job issues you allow her to become more at ease and less defensive, so that she is better able to make genuine contributions at the office. Together the two of you make levelheaded decisions.

YOUR SECOND-CHOICE SECONDARY CHEMISTRY

In this section, you will explore how to balance your relationship. Each of you will gain the self-control to protect the other from the consequences of excessive or impulsive actions.

Your Second Choice Calms Their First Choice

Your second choice naturally calms the charge-ahead agendas of your partner's first choice. Appreciate how more centered points of view give unbiased perspectives that put you back on track and diminish frustrations.

GREEN 2ND MEETS GREEN 1ST

As a second-choice green, you allow your first-choice green to see his sensitivity as a great gift. Your balanced sense of self is a constant source of strength to him. Give his worries a fair hearing, but don't let him become consumed by requirements. Keep his concerns from mushrooming.

As a first-choice green, you nurture your second-choice green. As you listen with concern, you encourage her to talk about the heart of the matter and make her environment more supportive. But when you are overwhelmed, you may appear indifferent or aloof. Together you acquire friends, opportunities, and possessions that make your lives more fulfilling.

PURPLE 2ND MEETS PURPLE 1ST

As a second-choice purple, you make your first-choice purple look at the facts. You tone down his drama by offering a more precise view of people and situations. Your more methodical personality calms your first-choice purple so that he can recognize what's most important in life.

As a passionate first-choice purple, you are a strong-willed, reflective strategist. You want to know why something was done before you act. You love to be challenged. Your second-choice purple appreciates how you see all of the possibilities. When you are overwhelmed, though, your assumptions can get in the way of understanding what's most important. Together you create realistic priorities.

ORANGE 2ND MEETS ORANGE 1ST

As a second-choice orange, you admire the way a first-choice orange creates a step-by-step process to produce a product, complete a task, or approach a life problem. When his critical questions become extreme, keep him on point by not taking them personally. Emphasize what works.

As a first-choice orange, you boldly separate yourself from your expectations in order to see the truth of a situation. Then you get things done without ruffling feathers. When you are disoriented, however, you may become overly critical, defensive, or apologetic. As a team, you're efficient and open-minded.

Your Second Choice Uplifts Their Third Choice

Your second choice provides a pillar of strength for your partner's third choice. Use this interaction to channel your frustrations into positive thoughts or, in a crisis, to teach your partner powerful self-truths about his or her sensitivity.

GREEN 2ND MEETS GREEN 3RD

As a second-choice green, help your third-choice green look inside to decipher exactly what he needs to find peace. Coach him not to expect others at home or work to know what he wants until he asks for it. When you spend time together, encourage him to be clear about how to make his life more comfortable.

As a third-choice green, you avoid understanding what you need. You are able to see exactly what you want only when you get emotionally upset. But your outburst won't upset your second-choice green, so don't be afraid to talk things out. Everyone benefits when you learn to ask for help—even coworkers who you have adopted as part of your family. Each of you is able to turn the other's concerns into supportive suggestions.

PURPLE 2ND MEETS PURPLE 3RD

As a second-choice purple, you see the hidden potential for your more methodical third-choice purple. Your considerations and balanced sense of logic allow him to be more comfortable, better able to take a risk. Without undue pressure, you encourage him to fulfill his true potential.

As a third-choice purple, you are very logical. Facts come before feelings. You disregard emotions in order to gain a more precise view of the people and situations around you. Become more open to your feelings and the knowledge you acquire will benefit you tremendously. The two of you are more ambitious and willing to risk doing something entirely new.

ORANGE 2ND MEETS ORANGE 3RD

As a second-choice orange, you ensure that your third-choice orange sees where things are going before he sets them in motion. You ask pointed questions that create reasonable expectations, so disappointments for your third-choice orange become fewer and he becomes less exhausted from spreading his energies too thin.

As a third-choice orange, you are open to the world. When you feel good, your naive approach to life charms even the most jaded. Pleasing others motivates you. But be careful. This is exactly where you get into trouble. If you promise less, you'll easily be able to deliver more. Together you can establish a realistic path that pleases both of you.

YOUR THIRD-CHOICE SECONDARY CHEMISTRY

Your third-choice connection highlights how you handle a crisis in romantic and workplace settings. Use these profiles to manage areas that you usually avoid. Otherwise, excessive or impulsive situations can keep you from attracting or maintaining fulfilling relationships.

Your Third Choice Meets Their First Choice

Your third choice both clashes with and empowers your partner's first choice. As you read, experience how their first choice can be a pillar of strength for your third choice. In a crisis, however, frustrations heighten sensitivity, and positive actions stall.

GREEN 3RD MEETS GREEN 1ST

As a third-choice green, be aware that your independent nature can make it difficult for you to reveal what you need, even to yourself. Your listening skills make it easier for you to see what works best. However, when a problem arises, you can feel as if you're all alone, without support.

As a first-choice green, you are able to identify what your partner needs, often before she knows what it is. Your supportive suggestions show her how to make her life more comfortable. Together you bond in one-on-one situations.

Romance and Dating: Love Tips

As a third-choice green, you find your first-choice green's attentiveness to your well-being to be very sexy. His concern will go a long way toward making you feel comfortable in your own skin. However, don't expect him to know how to best support you until you have dealt with your own feelings.

As a first-choice green, you can find it hard to understand your third-choice green's emotional outbursts. Since you effortlessly know what you want, why doesn't she have a clue? Coach your third-choice green to be more selfish about what's most important each day. Otherwise, she will put undue pressure on your relationship.

Workplace: Team-Building Tips

As a third-choice green, your independent nature allows you to work for long periods of time without any support. You know how to build a strong team—you even adopt coworkers as if they were your family. Don't let your attachments cloud your judgment or create unreasonable expectations. Others need to do what's best for them, not you.

A first-choice green's nurturing concern allows a third-choice green to recognize what she needs to get from others or her career. Appreciate how your concerned listening calms her thoughts and allows her to better handle other employee issues.

PURPLE 3RD MEETS PURPLE 1ST

A third-choice purple's methodical nature envisions a calm, neutral world where a first-choice purple can better manage information. However, your love of logical order can limit your own potential. The biggest dividends lie in your feelings and in risky situations. Reveal powerful possibilities by listening to your gut feelings and hearing out seemingly illogical ideas.

A first-choice purple's exciting, dramatic persona allows a third-choice purple to be more accepting of her emotional side. Your concerns empower her to see her true potential. However, your tendency to exaggerate feelings can make it difficult for you to evaluate a situation. Together you can see the realizable potential in each prospect.

Romance and Dating: Love Tips

As a third-choice purple, improve your relationship by discussing your feelings. Open up the lines of communication. So you had an argument—don't shut down. Take a few minutes to make a phone call; send an e-mail to an old friend; visit your parents. Reaching out is not your style, but it will make you feel more comfortable together.

A first-choice purple's exuberant energy keeps the romance flying high. However, at times, you need to cut the drama. Later, you will find that it is easier for your third-choice purple to deal with her softer, more vulnerable side. Create a safe refuge for her where she can express her feelings so that she learns to enjoy—and even be entertained by—your edgy, dramatic persona. You discover a renewed bond together.

Workplace: Team-Building Tips

A third-choice purple's methodical approach is treasured by a first-choice purple. It quickly puts an end to all his assumptions or exaggerated facts without any emotion. Valid information can then be used to draw successful conclusions.

As a first-choice purple, you help your third-choice purple to see her true career potential. At times, she views your venturing into uncharted waters as a waste of time and money. But don't let that slow you down. Charge ahead. Suggest possibilities beyond the status quo. Together you can combine profitable possibilities and a fact-based evaluation process to make excellent decisions.

ORANGE 3RD MEETS ORANGE 1ST

As a third-choice orange, you are emotionally open to the world. When you feel good, your naive approach to life charms even the most jaded. Your concerned, considerate persona makes an effort to please others, but it's also the source of your frustrations and your exhaustion from spreading your energies too thin. So be careful. Don't set your mind on doing something before you know exactly how you're going to do it.

As a first-choice orange, you are charismatic, dedicated,

affectionate, and big on hugs. You boldly detach from your expectations in order to see the truth of a situation. You ask analytical questions to avoid unreasonable expectations. As a team, you create an open awareness yet still see what is required before you act.

Romance and Dating: Love Tips

As a third-choice orange, don't expect your first-choice orange to do something that he disdains or to be someone other than himself. Remember that creating a great love together is all about having reasonable expectations. Honor your loved one's questions, even when he appears unnecessarily negative or defensive. Chances are your first-choice orange is all about getting you to be more realistic.

As a first-choice orange, soften your questions by expressing them out of concern: don't blow your third-choice orange away with undeniable facts. Her cheerful optimism will return to brighten your thoughts. If you constantly discuss your expectations together, you can craft true happiness.

Workplace: Team-Building Tips

As a third-choice orange, monitor what you expect from everyone around you. Apply the rule that "others are only going to do well what they enjoy" and don't expect otherwise. When you are overwhelmed, ask loads of questions instead of working until you drop. To your delight, you will discover that implementation tasks originally planned often are no longer needed or can be done more easily elsewhere.

As a first-choice orange, encourage your third-choice orange to set reasonable deadlines. Teach her to critically evaluate a project, in conjunction with other priorities, before she commits. With mutual respect, you two will become an open-minded team that tackles the right stuff.

Your Third Choice Meets Their Third Choice

Your third choice alternately calms and clashes with your partner's third choice. As you read, note how each of you bonds with the other's unfulfilled concerns and tends to overreact in a crisis. Simple awareness gives you the power to deal with issues before a crisis arises.

GREEN 3RD MEETS GREEN 3RD

Each of you usually appreciates the other's concern for how you're doing. You help each other recognize how you feel and exactly what's needed to make your life or the workday easier. When you are upset, however, deep-set emotions escape, and you somewhat recklessly express what you need. You feel as if you have been forgotten. Since you are both so alike, you fully understand each other's unexpected outbursts and are there to give support.

Relationship Tips

Being selfish would be a virtue for both of you. First of all, learn to be more specific with yourself about what you need. Then discuss it with your partner. You will both feel more at ease and less stressed. Otherwise, the pressure of constantly second-guessing what the other one wants will drive you both crazy.

PURPLE 3RD MEETS PURPLE 3RD

When you are together you are both very calm and methodical. People see your relationship as ideal. However, when you are upset, risky topics (those uncomfortable thoughts that you've been avoiding) flood your mind. You need to be alone to gather your thoughts. During this period, you can even stop speaking to your partner or avoid that taboo topic that needs to be discussed.

Relationship Tips

Even though you understand each other's ways, don't stay away too long. When the time is right, start a conversation about how you feel. If you expect your partner to initiate the reunion, get over it. Perhaps it's your turn to break the silence. Opening up will calm the waters and allow your relationship to flow smoothly again.

ORANGE 3RD MEETS ORANGE 3RD

The two of you create a world that at first seems perfect—almost surreal. Your expectations soar and spark fun events. When you are upset, though, you both simply try harder instead of confronting the real issues. Eventually, the situation will exhaust both of you. By not being realistic early on, you simply set each other up for failure.

Relationship Tips

Be on guard. Learn to recognize problems before you crash and burn. When you feel too serious, chances are you've set your mind on doing something that's headed nowhere. Get real. Address your frustrations with loads of questions about what's expected. Be up-front with each other about what you can and want to do. Greater satisfaction and less frustration will be your reward.

CHAPTER FIFTEEN

Achromatic Connection

Your Hopes and Fears

It's choice—not chance—that determines your destiny.

—JEAN NIDETCH

Black, white, and brown indicate your core essence: your hopes and fears. In reading about your achromatic connections with your friends, family, romantic partners, and coworkers, you will learn how to make good decisions together. Review your achromatic color ranking on page 16 before you begin.

In this interactive chapter, consider your thoughtful, contemplative moments. Tune in to the voice inside your head, especially when pressure is forcing change. Listen and you will hear how you balance the benefits and drawbacks of each consideration. Then look beyond what's being said to experience each other's hopes and fears.

Note how distance, both physical and mental, plays a part in your unique negotiating style. For example, a first-choice black, who has subjective, emotional concerns, stands too close; a first-choice white, who has objective, problem-solving concerns, stands back; and a first-choice brown, who maintains a grounded perspective, stands neither too far away nor too close.

Celebrate your most passionate deep-rooted concerns. Relish the innate way in which each of you balances the other. Then dig deep and confront together whatever inhibits your most desired pursuits. Discovering the underlying force behind your hopes and fears will ground your concerns so that you will be better able to solve each other's greatest dilemmas together.

YOUR FIRST-CHOICE ACHROMATIC CHEMISTRY

Your favorite achromatic choices mix to make contributions and match to create agreement. They indicate how you make decisions together. They also reveal the way you express your most passionate innermost concerns.

Your First Choice Matches Their First Choice

If the two of you share the same achromatic color preference, you either firmly agree or firmly disagree. In a crisis, you can even see in your partner exactly what you dislike in yourself. As you read, appreciate how you both set priorities and arrive at decisions in the same way.

BLACK 1ST MEETS BLACK 1ST

Key Words: Emotional, Focused, Loyal

Together: You hold on dearly to what's important

Each of you genuinely appreciates how loyal the other is to those he or she cares about. You both feel good about the decisions and sacrifices you make on behalf of each other. Your mutual sincerity makes you both feel important. This creates a powerful bond and nonstop memorable experiences. However, when you are upset, those feelings may become disruptive: both of you turn stubborn, or even paranoid, expecting the worst.

Family and Friends: Supportive Tips

Don't allow your family member's strong opinions to keep you from being close. Chances are the two of you are more alike than you admit. Acknowledge his point of view and he will hear everything you say, even when he doesn't appear to be listening. The next day pay close attention to how he has adopted your way and made it his own.

Romance and Dating: Love Tips

You both adore each other's warmth, intensity, loyalty, and dedication. Because you see eye to eye on most issues your union is one of unquestionable trust. When one of you is feeling down, support your partner. However, back off in a disagreement. Don't lock horns. Being stubborn or bringing up past disappointments fuels exaggerated comments or circumstances. Don't take personally what is said in an argument. Simply give your loved one comfort by not getting all wrapped up in your own emotional agendas. After you cool off and settle down, you'll find the words to get you both back in each other's arms.

Workplace: Team-Building Tips

Your coworkers are loyal to both of you. You admire each other's strong-willed focus, but you don't listen to each other in a crisis. At first, you both believe your way is best; the irony is that you may both be right. Back off: restate your goals and concerns. Write everything down. Then assemble a very focused, detailed plan that incorporates all the elements necessary for success. Remember: the goal is to win; it doesn't matter in the end whose suggestion was the best.

WHITE 1ST MEETS WHITE 1ST

Key Words: Objective, Curious, Analytical

Together: You turn dilemmas into solutions

Each of you gives the other the freedom you need in life. But you use your shared curiosity to solve problems. You admire each other's independence, and this empowers both of you to stay focused on your separate futures without undue interference. You both need space in a crisis. Getting you two to agree may be a struggle.

Family and Friends: Supportive Tips

Things work best with family and friends if you share common interests, such as favorite sport teams or television shows. Keep your concerns moving in the same direction for the most part by scheduling one-on-one time together. When a disagreement occurs, you both step back to gain perspective; you may even try to see things from the other person's point of view. Resolve conflicts right away by discussing either what you will do or what you want to do. Otherwise, sensitive issues will make you both increasingly uncomfortable.

Romance and Dating: Love Tips

Although each of you is highly tolerant of the other's differences, you both require lots of elbow room. The two of you are involved in a million things—but you should find time to do things *together*. Arrange regular dates to keep your romantic connection strong. Otherwise, your life apart from your partner will unravel when a crisis arises. Don't spend too much time away: you risk turning your mate into a mere acquaintance.

Workplace: Team-Building Tips

Your objective, curious, analytical connection is a problem-solving powerhouse. Each of you admires the other's ability to work independently and stay focused on his or her job without interference. When a disagreement arises, however, you both tend to back off rather than confront the situation head-on. Brainstorm before you waste a lot of energy. Ensure that each of you has an opportunity to propose not only a solution to fix the current problem but also an innovative overview of the task at hand.

BROWN 1ST MEETS BROWN 1ST

Key Words: Aware, Authentic, Compassionate

Together: You create action-oriented excitement

Your compassionate awareness creates an environment in which each of you can appreciate the pleasures of life. High-energy experiences and comfortable situations define your relationship: you both exist in a world entirely your own. You talk about fun upcoming events that you both enjoy, better ways to get tasks accomplished, how to make your home more comfortable, and how to support loved ones. To others, both of you are free of illusions and aware of consequences.

Family and Friends: Supportive Tips

One activity after another with family and friends consumes your day. Puttering around the house, going to the gym, helping a friend, or simply doing whatever feels good at the moment commands your focus. Under stress, however, each of you becomes concerned only about pent-up desires. Sensations can even overrule logic. Take the time to sincerely appreciate how much support each of you gives to the other every day. This realization will rechannel your desires into more worthwhile causes.

Romance and Dating: Love Tips

Action excites the two of you. Keep the fire roaring: don't let career or family demands interrupt your action connection. If you feel compulsively driven to accomplish something, be wary. You can destroy your ability to be truly intimate and alienate your partner. Take the time to listen to each other's sincere, heartfelt concerns.

Workplace: Team-Building Tips

You accomplish goals together with minimal waste of resources. Things are done right the first time. Your task-oriented personas turn even the most mundane situations into fun. However, nonstop action makes you spin your wheels. If you become consumed by a project, you may leave your partner out on a ledge. So, no matter how dire the situation, don't take on more than you can handle.

Your First Choice Mixes with Their First Choice

If the two of you prefer different achromatic colors, you complement each other's point of view. As you read, appreciate how you both effortlessly gain insight into the pros and cons of each situation.

BLACK 1ST MEETS WHITE 1ST

Key Words: Emotional, Focused, Loyal meets

Objective, Curious, Analytical

Together: You make great decisions

As a black, you talk about your feelings. The emotion a white hears in your voice makes him feel more comfortable in his own skin. Your dedicated concerns ease even his most irritating or illogical feelings. A white objectively calms an emotional black so that she can appreciate logical options.

A white's menu of suggestions offers a black new ways to solve issues or use resources. Be aware when you are upset. Your searching for the perfect solution can make you lose focus or make others feel that you don't believe in or appreciate them. The two of you make thoughtful, considerate decisions together.

Family and Friends: Supportive Tips

As a black, you are proud of your white's ambition and accomplishments, and appreciate his constant barrage of problem-solving suggestions. Family and friends adore your care and concern, even if they don't acknowledge it as often as you'd like. Their world would be a colder place without you.

As a white, you help your black chill. Your constant advice gets her to look before she leaps. You appreciate your black's loyalty. It makes you feel safe, and you are thus better able to express your own feelings. Her devotion to the family and your helpful counsel make life easier and everything more fun.

Romance and Dating: Love Tips

As a black, you need large doses of togetherness to thrive. However, get used to the fact that your white needs freedom to do her own thing. Even though this can be frustrating and makes you too needy at times, it can also be very sexy. In fact, black-white is the classic yin-yang relationship—an ongoing balancing act.

As a white, you require a little "loving" distance, even when your black is pressing for closeness. The two of you clash when he mistakes your cooler style for indifference or you feel that he's hovering. Here's a trick for handling your black when he gets a bit intense: gently touch his arm as you look into his eyes. Calm him down by showing him that you understand and care about his feelings.

Workplace: Team-Building Tips

As a black, your direct, concerned persona allows your white to pull his thoughts together. Once your decisive nature expresses what needs to be done, your coworker considers all available problem-solving options. Opinions that you assume to be facts can actually be turned into viable considerations.

As a white, you pull back from a situation in order to view it objectively. Your black, in turn, pushes forward. You may feel rushed or that you need more information before you come to a conclusion. At times, you think your black makes decisions too quickly and you withdraw even more. The result is either a clash or great brainstorming. The two of you make good decisions together in the workplace.

BLACK 1ST MEETS BROWN 1ST

Key Words: Emotional, Focused, Loyal meets Aware, Authentic, Compassionate

Together: You accomplish difficult tasks

As a black, you challenge your brown to contemplate what's most important. Your concern encourages him to accumulate more wealth or to feel the depth and breadth of your relationship. Together the two of you spark action-oriented energy. In a crisis, your emotions can discount practical solutions—a major frustration to your brown.

As a brown, your practical concerns keep your black from hitting brick walls. Your intuitiveness teaches her to come back down to earth and concentrate on current practicalities, not unobtainable expectations. However, you can become consumed by what you're doing and either miss the point or make your black feel like an afterthought.

Family and Friends: Supportive Tips

As a black, appreciate your brown's unwavering support. Otherwise, you may wound him, and he will feel less important and unappreciated. If he is overly obsessed with helping others or consumed by what he's doing, don't pout or whine about it. Instead, tell him how much you need him: he will soon get back on track.

As a brown, use your intuitiveness to coach your black to concentrate on current practicalities and to not take things so personally. Urge her to be more levelheaded: ground her concerns and give her the latitude to be at ease even when she's having a somewhat moody moment. You will make excellent decisions together without upsetting the status quo.

Romance and Dating: Love Tips

For browns: to understand how you gain insight in your romantic relationships, you need to choose another achromatic color. Do you prefer black or white? After you've selected your preference, turn to the appropriate page in this chapter to read your personalized love tips.

Workplace: Team-Building Tips

As a black, use your focus to keep your brown on track. Remind him of the goal when he becomes consumed with implementing projects or supporting current programs. But be careful not to discount your brown's need to experience things before he gives you his opinion. If you make him feel unappreciated, he will lose respect for you.

As a brown, teach your black to be more practical; explain the need for experimentation to avoid wasting time or money. Don't become engrossed in endless projects: you risk leaving your black without your support and missing the point. As a team, you generate action-oriented enthusiasm that gets the job done right.

WHITE 1ST MEETS BROWN 1ST

Key Words: Objective, Curious, Analytical meets

Aware, Authentic, Compassionate

Together: You fascinate each other

As a white, you appreciate how your brown grounds both your relationship and the world around you. Your steady flow of suggestions takes your brown's thoughts into new realms. He feels a burst of freedom and gains the foresight to stop supporting situations and others that don't appreciate him. In a personal crisis, however, your emphasis on what he needs to do seems to discount what he's done.

As a brown, your dedication and sharp awareness are a constant source of stimulation for a white. Your observations create an ongoing stream of useful information. You make each day fun and full of action. When you don't feel appreciated, however, you either devote yourself to others who need you or become preoccupied with high-energy activities. This shift may leave your white feeling unnoticed and undervalued.

Family and Friends: Supportive Tips

As a brown, you make your white feel secure through your ability to maintain steadfast concern. Be proud of how your white is better able to feel close to others because of your support. If you think your white doesn't notice that you're around, simply back off and wait. He will approach you with an entirely new appreciation for your contribution.

As a white, don't let your constant flood of considerations distract you from your brown's supportive assistance. If you feel indifferent toward your brown's contributions, she will become selfish or lazy or devote herself to others who need her more than you do. Together you create a fun, supportive, ever-evolving, highly charged relationship.

Romance and Dating: Love Tips

For browns: to understand how you gain insight in your romantic relationships, you need to choose another achromatic color. Do you prefer black or white? After you've selected your preference, turn to the appropriate page in this chapter to read your personalized love tips.

Workplace: Team-Building Tips

As a white, you view your brown's down-to-earth thinking as being limited, even simple. This is his nature; perhaps you need to make it yours as well. If you use your brown's grounded concerns to ensure that what you're attempting to do will actually work, you'll get it right the first time.

As a brown, you are a natural at managing high-volume activities, task-oriented projects, or physically supportive roles, thanks to your dedication, sharp awareness, and keen observations. Focus your practical remarks on achieving the goal. A white-brown duo's practical, winning suggestions solve problems.

YOUR SECOND-CHOICE ACHROMATIC CHEMISTRY

In this section, you will explore how you and your partner balance each other's decisions. Take pride in how each of you inspires, calms, uplifts, and directs each other without wounding egos.

Your Second Choice Calms Their First Choice

Use your second-choice composure to strengthen your partner's first-choice passionate, hasty considerations. Discover how to get more done with less effort.

BLACK 2ND MEETS BLACK 1ST

As a second-choice black, encourage your first-choice black to think more rationally and not to get so tangled up in his emotions. Enable him to stand back and prioritize what's important. His strong opinions will melt into reasonable expectations and dismiss the frustration derived from his tendencies to overachieve.

As a first-choice black, appreciate the value of your relationship. Heed your second-choice black's advice when the impetuous, forceful part of you overdoes it. Listen to her recommendations not to take people and events too seriously, especially when you are upset. Together you can cut to the truth, gauge a promising future, and still dearly treasure each memory.

WHITE 2ND MEETS WHITE 1ST

As a second-choice white, encourage your first-choice white to craft solutions by focusing on the objective. This process will make him more decisive and encourage a more precise analysis that takes into account long-term consequences.

As a first-choice white, you initially avoid connecting to situations or people so that you can assess all available options. Encourage your second-choice white to choose from your menu of suggestions to help her reconsider problems thoroughly and then solve them. When you are upset, your search for the perfect solution can prevent your partner from appreciating all your contributions. Sometimes you lose sight of what you most value. As a team, you objectively assess your world and present empowering solutions to real-life problems.

BROWN 2ND MEETS BROWN 1ST

As a second-choice brown, honor your first-choice brown for his contributions. Does his work complete him? Do the people he supports truly appreciate his efforts? Create an atmosphere of exciting, authentic energy for him.

As a first-choice brown, you live life to the fullest and savor the pleasures of the world around you. Use your powerful awareness to identify exactly what works best for you and your partner and how to get it. When you are upset, your own needs consume you and you neglect your invested interests. A brown duo efficiently and successfully completes projects.

Your Second Choice Uplifts Their Third Choice

Described below is an area where the second choice's ability to confront issues that have been avoided by the third choice saves time and money. Encourage discussions to arrive at common-sense decisions. Expressing a question as a concern will dispel defensiveness.

BLACK 2ND MEETS BLACK 3RD

As a second-choice black, use your concerns to get a third-choice black more in touch with his emotional side. Don't let his logic intimidate you. Charge ahead. Use your balanced, emotional good sense to let your third-choice black know if coming changes will really fit his needs or impart value.

As a third-choice black, the emotional you makes rational, unemotional decisions. Using only logic, you can see where others are excessive and inconsistent. Give them your unbiased perspective. Use your facts and levelheaded ways to advise your second-choice black and get her on the right track. Don't forget to show her your dedication as well. Your logical appraisals improve the effectiveness of the home and the workplace.

WHITE 2ND MEETS WHITE 3RD

As a second-choice white, you enable a third-choice white to see his life more objectively. When the two of you are together, your empowering suggestions prompt your partner to devise solutions and resolve personal issues.

As a third-choice white, you make others feel that they belong. Your very presence inspires people so that success seamlessly follows. Even though your flood of suggestions truly supports your second-choice white, seek advice from her when trouble is brewing. Don't panic in a crisis; instead, weigh alternatives to give yourself the breathing room to know what's best. As a team, you make the best of each situation yet still know when to move on.

BROWN 2ND MEETS BROWN 3RD

As a centered second-choice brown, you are very stable and down-to-earth. Use your natural skills to identify what is authentic. Coach your third-choice brown on how to avoid the frustration of unobtainable expectations.

As a third-choice brown, constantly ground yourself by accepting both the demands of a situation and the needs of others before you act. Don't fight the natural flow of human nature. Keep things real by not making unrealistic demands of yourself, your family, or your coworkers. You will feel more complete and realize how to make your lives together simpler and more fun.

YOUR THIRD-CHOICE ACHROMATIC CHEMISTRY

Your third-choice connection highlights the issues you both usually avoid. As you read, consider your most powerful emotions. Honor your feelings with understanding before you try to apply logic to them. Otherwise, excessive or impulsive situations can erupt.

Your 3rd Choice Meets Their 1st Choice

Your third choice both clashes with and empowers your partner's first choice. As you read, experience how their first choice can be a pillar of strength for your third choice. In a crisis, however, frustrations heighten sensitivity and positive actions stall.

BLACK 3RD MEETS BLACK 1ST

As a third-choice black, you create a calm, stable feeling for your first-choice black through your no-nonsense perspective. You give him the information he needs to solve problems.

When a crisis arises, however, you prefer to concentrate solely on the relevant facts, not your own emotions. As a result, your first-choice black tends to see you as aloof.

Yet your relationship is uniquely complementary. As a first-choice black, you are comfortable with your emotions and voice them without hesitation. Your constant expression of how you feel adds excitement and adventure to your third-choice black's life. By dwelling on your emotions, you make it difficult to be objective, however, and it becomes impossible for your third-choice black to hear you. Together each of you balances the other's emotions.

Family and Friends: Supportive Tips

As a third-choice black, keep your first-choice black's emotions in check. Use your powerful logic to place relevant facts foremost in his thoughts. Don't let his stubborn appearance deflate your efforts. He does absorb your comments. By the next day, his opinions sound very much like yours.

As a first-choice black, appreciate your third-choice black's ability to give you "just the facts." Don't be judgmental, even when she appears to be cold or uncaring. Instead, ask her how she feels, and don't stop until you hear a heartfelt response. As a team, you arrive at a clear understanding of the best solution.

Workplace: Team-Building Tips

As a third-choice black, you are viewed by your first-choice black as disrupting projects that are headed in the right direction. But deliver your message anyway, out of concern for the project and your coworkers. You'll find that the first-choice black, however, cannot hear what's said without emotions. It upsets you when your first-choice black voices opinions without logic to back them up.

As a first-choice black, you are comfortable with your

emotions and have no problem expressing them at work. Your sincerity adds focus and prioritizes important concerns. However, when an idea is cemented in your mind, it is important to listen to your third-choice black's advice. Consider what she is proposing without feeling obligated to comply. If you do, a new and better method or way to achieve a goal may result. You make great decisions together.

WHITE 3RD MEETS WHITE 1ST

As a third-choice white, honor your first-choice white's need for space. Without a buffer, he will feel as if he is losing a part of himself and withdraw even more—such a shift will frighten you. Instead, know that the emotional discomfort you feel when your first-choice white backs away is just temporary. This realization will allow you to bond rather than grow apart.

As a first-choice white, you avoid being too close so that you can objectively assess all available options. Appreciate how your third-choice white, on the other hand, needs to make what's been decided or done okay. As a team, you can start something new while still using what's already working.

Family and Friends: Supportive Tips

As a third choice-white, pull your family member's or friend's life together. Use your concerned questions to make your first-choice white feel good about himself. Listen to his suggestions; you don't have to make them fit into your life, but learn from them. They may reveal long-term consequences that are holding you back.

As a first-choice white, be there for your third-choice white, especially in an emotional crisis. Your calm, rational, problem-solving skills open new doors and revitalize her life.

Appreciate that the issues you handle well she simply can't handle, and vice versa. Together you create a close-knit connection.

Workplace: Team-Building Tips

As a third-choice white, you make the impossible possible. Appreciate how your very presence makes everyone feel part of the team. However, in a crisis, honor your first-choice white's objective suggestions. Otherwise, your fear of destroying the unity of the group or the integrity of the project may impede progress.

As a first-choice white, you avoid being too close to your third-choice white in order to objectively evaluate all the alternatives. This gives you the power to solve problems, even in a crisis. Present your solutions to your third-choice white, even if she isn't receptive. If you remain objective, you will put her at ease so that she can do what's best.

BROWN 3RD MEETS BROWN 1ST

As a third-choice brown, you learn to listen to your first-choice brown's rationality. He will teach you to accept situations and human behavior as they are—nothing less and nothing more. If you listen unconditionally, you will gain an appreciation for why someone acts a certain way or understand why a task needs to be completed to a particular specification. Accept the facts, especially the ones that feel like a cold shower. They will diminish your frustrations and make you more of a winner.

As a first-choice brown, use your awareness to get things grounded and keep your relationship authentic. Cut out excessive expectations and inform your third-choice brown about the consequences of her actions, but be careful. Keep your concerns relevant by caring most about those who care about you. Don't overlook relevant long-term issues because of your hyperactivity. Simplify your lives together and direct your actions toward an exciting future.

Family and Friends: Supportive Tips

A third-choice brown's determination against all odds is admirable, but it's also his downfall. Listen to your first-choice brown's advice. Isn't he telling you that a situation or person is just that way? Learn not to fantasize about what you can't change. Ironically, you'll see how to make improvements.

As a first-choice brown, keep your third-choice brown from being immersed in issues or situations that just won't work out. Teach her that there is no way to know how others really feel until she's walked in their shoes. Your life journey together becomes an adventurous blend between the abstract and the very real world.

Workplace: Team-Building Tips

As a third-choice brown, teach your first-choice brown to acknowledge his contributions and to channel his energy toward situations where his efforts will be appreciated. Be cautious. Don't accept his facts as the final word. Instead, use them in combination with what you already know to fix things.

As a first-choice brown, your awareness stabilizes your third-choice brown. Your obvious, simple, practical points of view keep her from squandering time and energy. Give her constant reality-based advice to enhance her control. Rely on all-encompassing facts that solve problems when working together, and both of you will prosper.

Your Third Choice Meets Their Third Choice

As you read, note how you both react to situations in the same way. Each of you bonds with the other's unfulfilled concerns. In a crisis, you are consumed by issues and experiences that you usually avoid.

BLACK 3RD MEETS BLACK 3RD

Each of you appreciates the other's solid approach to life. You enjoy rational conversations, without the intrusion of confusing emotions. If a disagreement about a common goal or decision occurs, however, your relationship will momentarily stumble. Both of you will be consumed by your feelings—those illogical distractions that make you confront your inner self.

Relationship Tips

Let your emotions also speak by making it a point to discuss your feelings every day. Learn to be less factual with your partner, to sit back, relax, and let your emotions breathe life back into you. At first the flood of feelings will make you uncomfortable, but later on you will marvel at your new inner drive and strengthened bond. Information that you needed for success will also be revealed.

WHITE 3RD MEETS WHITE 3RD

You create a strong sense of security for each other. Your close-knit relationship makes you both feel less alone and more protected. Problems occur when you're confronted with changes that affect your relationship. One of you must retreat for a while to understand how to move forward. The other may interpret the current situation as disapproval and become defensive.

Relationship Tips

Accept that occasionally backing off from your relationship is healthy. Even though it doesn't feel good, some distance will be very productive and restorative for both of you. Rest assured that when you reconnect, your bond will be revitalized. At work, not needing to make everything or everyone work together as a team is productive on occasion, as well.

BROWN 3RD MEETS BROWN 3RD

The two of you create a world that is more about dreams than the real world. Your determination is admirable. You ask a lot of others—and perhaps even more of yourselves. At times, your unrealistic expectations can indeed create an outcome that you first thought unobtainable. But be careful when tackling those things that others wouldn't even attempt. You can set yourself up for failure. Before you waste your efforts or money, accept the brutal reality of each situation and your partner's capabilities, or you risk creating major frustrations.

Relationship Tips

Be more grounded. Help each other take things as they come. Before you create an expectation, accept the hard facts of each situation and what your partner enjoys doing as his self-truth. Don't go against the natural flow of life or your relationship. Then both of you will be more successful in your aspirations and more in sync with each other's lives.

CHAPTER SIXTEEN

Intermediate Connection

Taking on the World

Diplomacy is the art of letting someone else get your way.

—ANONYMOUS

In this chapter, you will discover how key personality traits contribute to your connection with friends, family, romantic partners, and coworkers. Contemplate how your concerns—even when unspoken—engage the world. Review your intermediate color selections on page 16–17 before you begin.

These energized hues show how you both voice requests to fulfill your desires. For example, lime green, indigo, and red-orange preferences push forward to take action. On the other hand, magenta, teal, and gold preferences lean back and thoughtfully consider what's required. Both styles can be equally assertive.

As you read about each category with your partner, you will find out how you boost each other's self-esteem, enthusiasm, and creativity. Learn how thoughts and ideas are crafted into clever ways to accomplish a task or approach each other with a request. Gain invaluable insights into the rewards and consequences of your interpersonal connection.

Are you introspective or outgoing, empathetic or ambitious, a resourceful idea person or a logical reasoner? Have fun watching your partner act out the characteristics of these easy-to-spot hues. Determine simple ways to fine-tune your natural talents and open up each other's lives.

HOW YOUR PREFERENCES MESH

If the two of you share the same intermediate color combination, you have a window of understanding to how your partner approaches certain issues and situations. Your partner's considerations are much like yours.

If you and your partner choose different combinations, you will discover areas where each of you can learn marvelous new skills from the other. Your partner's considerations will complement yours.

Lime Green and Magenta

Lime green and magenta are the colors of spiritual regeneration. A lime green's introspective thoughts inspire new beginnings, while a magenta's open-to-the-world curiosity sparks opportunities.

LIME GREEN PREFERENCE MEETS MAGENTA PREFERENCE

Key Words: Introspective, Logical, Assertive meets

Enthusiastic, Inspiring, Optimistic

Passion: To be inspired

Together: You ignite each other's passions

As a lime green, ask logical questions that identify what is missing from both of your lives. This process will allow both of you to better communicate by confronting underlying issues before they wreak havoc. You encourage your magenta to be committed before he invests his time and energy in someone or something.

As a magenta, use your open-minded enthusiasm to create new situations and opportunities for both of you. Curiosity provides the spark that reveals new possibilities and attracts excitement and projects, sometimes more than you can manage. Together you inspire each other.

Family and Friends: Supportive Tips

As a lime green, use your time with your magenta to focus on your needs: window-shop before you reject or buy into either a person or a project. Learn how your magenta uses curiosity to open new doors, make new friends, and attract support.

As a magenta, pay attention to your recurring thoughts. Identify the issues that are holding you back: they indicate how you waste time and energy. Each of you inspires the other to stay headed in the right direction.

Romance and Dating: Love Tips

On the surface, a lime green seems to be the one who is in control and making all the decisions: he has the final word. But in reality, a magenta's exciting, behind-the-scenes support is what keeps the attraction magnetic. As a lime green, don't expect to turn on your magenta unless you offer something new. Magentas love high energy and new situations. So loosen up and have some fun.

As a magenta, use your seductive body language and inquisitive nature to fascinate your lime green. At first your lime green uses his "good sense" to keep your relationship from becoming too close. In the end, however, emotions win out, and you will find yourself in the driver's seat—for once, more logical about your romantic connection than your lime green, who is now all wrapped up in his feelings. Use your adventurous spirit to make your lime green's life more magical. But don't expect him to be enthusiastic until he knows how it feels to be with you. Together you keep your relationship just spicy enough.

Workplace: Team-Building Tips

As a lime green, you are a logical, quick-thinking self-starter on the job. You ask your magenta pertinent, no-nonsense questions. Use your logic to guide projects and confront work tasks, even the tough ones, before they become real problems. However, when there is no apparent solution, you may become bottlenecked with too much information or miss the point.

As a magenta, inspire your lime green by getting her to be more open when it comes to unfamiliar situations or unusual opportunities. This encouragement will get her head out of the clouds and into the real world. Your workplace passion is starting projects: whenever possible you delegate others to complete them. You need to learn to finish what you start, however, or an all-out war will begin. You make effective decisions together and get more accomplished.

LIME GREEN PREFERENCE MEETS LIME GREEN PREFERENCE

Key Words: Introspective, Logical, Assertive

Passion: To know exactly what's needed

Together: Your questions keep each other on track

Each of you admires the other's logic, honesty, and vulnerability. Together you are a truly dynamic duo. Your pertinent questions enable each other to accomplish a task or solve a problem.

You make your partner bolder by encouraging him to jump in and just do it. However, when taken together, your forthright comments are a bit off-putting. Learn to step back and be more considerate. And remember: even if you don't voice your concerns, a stern or worried look on your face will convey to your partner disapproval or doubt in his ability.

Relationship Tips

Lime green lovers are assertive and equally bold. During a quarrel, consider the consequences before you speak. Don't jump to conclusions; instead, ask more questions in a non-threatening way. Dig deeper and reconsider your partner's action from a cause-and-effect perspective. Otherwise, in a crunch you will endlessly second-guess each other or end up making someone else (your mother-in-law, perhaps?) angry. Iron it out the first time by not turning suspicions into assumptions.

MAGENTA PREFERENCE MEETS MAGENTA PREFERENCE

Key Words: Enthusiastic, Inspiring, Optimistic

Passion: To create with a smile

Together: Your openness creates constant opportunities

You are both enthusiastic, and it's a source of inspiration. If you relish each other's spirited attitude, your relationship will be ever joyful. Take the time to seek out remarkable people. Others will flock to you, and exciting events will occur every day.

Relationship Tips

Learn from how your partner's curiosity enlists support and sparks opportunities. Use this knowledge to create romantic rendezvous, solve misunderstandings, and give support. Your magnetic chemistry inspires those around the two of you to take on projects that they would otherwise have never attempted. When stressed, you both become more confrontational, and new projects stall. Expect one of you to complete an unfinished project that you both believe is boring. Before you decide to start a new adventure, make sure that you really want to see it through.

Teal and Red-Orange

Teal and red-orange are the colors of self-esteem. A teal diplomatically requests approval from others, whereas a red-orange honors the individual's concerns.

TEAL PREFERENCE MEETS RED-ORANGE PREFERENCE

Key Words: Empathetic, Diplomatic, Supportive meets

Self-respectful, Individualist, Personable

Passion: To feel important

Together: You achieve self-realization

As a teal, you are sure-footed, with an unrelenting belief in yourself and your relationships. When a red-orange preference is down and out, you stand firm in support of his future. By actively listening to his side of the story and diplomatically providing feedback, you give him confidence. Your strong endorsement gives your red-orange the impetus to fight for himself.

As a red-orange, you ensure that everyone around you is honored and respected through your unselfish devotion. Your tuned-in observations keep your teal true to herself, and she is then better able to dispel concerns about what others think. If you learn from her diplomacy skills, you will "fit in" better, become less defensive, and acknowledge points of view that will expand your world.

Family and Friends: Supportive Tips

As a teal, you encourage your red-orange to believe in his dreams and appreciate his own contributions. In turn, your red-orange encourages you to have a stronger sense of self and not be so concerned with the appreciation of your peers.

Just by being your independent red-orange self, you give your teal the inner strength to be more authentic and to appreciate true warmth and love. From your teal, you learn to not take things so personally. Together you know where best to place your faith.

Romance and Dating: Love Tips

As a teal, you believe in your red-orange, and that makes him feel more accepted. Your honest observations help him to gauge his own worth—to believe in himself. However, when your red-orange is championing his own causes, he may become distant and forget about you.

As a red-orange, you make your teal feel as if she is the most important person in the world. As she basks in your love she becomes less preoccupied with what others think. The two of you build each other's self-esteem.

Workplace: Team-Building Tips

As a teal, you make your red-orange feel more a part of the team by believing in him. Use your honest observations and tactful communication skills to cheer on your red-orange. Give him an incentive to do a better job. Your red-orange's respect for your contributions will allow you to feel good about yourself in return.

As a red-orange, you feel less skeptical and defensive when

partnered with a teal. Her concerns make you appreciate your own workplace victories more. In return, you transform your teal's "I must do what others expect" selflessness into reasonable expectations. Working together, you gain the power to appreciate and build each other's true worth.

TEAL PREFERENCE MEETS TEAL PREFERENCE

Key Words: Empathetic, Diplomatic, Supportive

Passion: To believe in your dreams

Together: Your listening makes wishes come true

You are both exceedingly considerate. The diplomatic communication skills of a teal duo are unparalleled. You both listen to and support each other's dreams, which gives you the confidence to be more successful. As a team, you make everything appear perfect. In your mind, there is nothing that you and your partner can't do. People flock to you for reassurance.

Relationship Tips

Reality can be rough when your relationship hits an obstacle. Don't feel downtrodden; instead, if you recognize this time as a period for rebuilding, your success will be even greater. Feeling a need to keep up appearances only interferes with your ability to formulate solutions. If you are more concerned about what needs to be done than what others will think about your behavior, you will make your original wishes come true.

RED-ORANGE PREFERENCE MEETS RED-ORANGE PREFERENCE

Key Words: Self-respectful, Individualist, Personable

Passion: To be respected for who you are

Together: You have the inner strength to be yourself

Each of you honors the other's authenticity, honesty, and devotion. Being yourself is key: ignore what others say about you. It is also important to be appreciated and respected for who you are. You learn to value each other's powerful sense of personal integrity.

Relationship Tips

In your world, mutual self-respect is your foremost concern. So, tempers will quickly flare in a high-stress situation if either of you becomes too critical of the other. Chances are your partner felt his opinion was belittled. Apologize and rephrase your question in a less personal way; focus more on what's needed than what was done. Then remind yourselves that honoring each other is what's most important.

Indigo and Gold

Indigo and gold are the colors that reveal how you finesse the world to unleash your creative potential. An indigo is an idea person who creates orchestrated plans; a golds gathers resources to make something from nothing.

INDIGO PREFERENCE MEETS GOLD PREFERENCE

Key Words: Enterprising, Conceptual, Self-confident meets Passionate, Inventive, Playful

Passion: To create something original

Together: You communicate the entire creative process

As an indigo, you love to come up with a plan. For you, the ultimate high is figuring out how to make your ideas a reality and then making them happen. Others are empowered by your self-confidence. Your abilities to evaluate how to best use resources and to skillfully plan merge to create original products, services, or better ways to enjoy your life together.

As a gold, you know how to marshal resources for their ultimate purpose. Using your probing curiosity, you uncover what you want and proceed to get it. When you have the time to playfully associate the usability of resources, you create original things.

Family and Friends: Supportive Tips

As an indigo, you become disoriented when your adventurous gold shakes up your rigorous schedules. Isn't this exactly what you need? Encourage your gold favorite to devise a fun plan and expect to set aside your responsibilities for a while. It's okay to allocate downtime for relaxation.

As a gold, use your passionate persona to make things happen. But should you find yourself without the flexibility to make a planned event more playful, you become resentful. Even though your indigo's plans might achieve the desired results, share your thoughts with her ahead of time. As a team, you will gain the vision to recognize which ideas work best for the both of you.

Romance and Dating: Love Tips

As an indigo, you love to make plans; however, your gold will make your itinerary more playful. Don't feel left out when he becomes absorbed in the world around him. That's how he discovers his own essence.

As a gold, you love to experience events like white-water rafting, camping, and games with kids for the fun of it. Your indigo, on the other hand, explores her creativity by constantly planning dinner parties or vacations or by being a host. Don't expect an indigo to become as immersed in your projects as you are. To generate new ideas, she lives more inside her head. Together you create nonstop fun that always seems to work out.

Workplace: Team-Building Tips

As an indigo, you love to decide in advance exactly how you will accomplish the day's work. If you give your gold some slack, he will show you shortcuts—how to better incorporate materials or streamline procedures to ease the workload. You will save time and money.

As a passionate gold, you demand a stimulating work environment and the time to enjoy it. Your probing curiosity drives you to uncover what you need, eliminate waste, and complete your task. Resources coalesce to create clever, inventive possibilities. However, your approach to projects sometimes overwhelms your indigo's need for a more focused plan. Together you efficiently make ideas a reality.

INDIGO PREFERENCE MEETS INDIGO PREFERENCE

Key Words: Enterprising, Conceptual, Self-confident

Passion: To fix everything

Together: You orchestrate successful plans

Each of you admires how the other goes after what he wants. Building your dreams together creates an exciting energy between the two of you. You encourage each other's "outside the box" thinking about the future. Your devoted attention and skillful planning keeps your relationship on track, unless your plans become excessively rigid. Remember that even the best ideas need to be constantly modified in order to be implemented successfully.

Relationship Tips

Each of you has different expectations and strategies for getting ahead. Both approaches may work equally well, so engage in an open discussion. Otherwise, an unnecessary turf war will result. Does it really matter whose idea is best? Develop a strategy together, but don't compromise essentials. Ensure success by reconsidering your original plan every week or so. Revise it, if necessary, based on the latest developments.

GOLD PREFERENCE MEETS GOLD PREFERENCE

Key Words: Passionate, Inventive, Playful

Passion: To see value in everything

Together: You create something from nothing

Golds interact playfully. By investigating the world around you together, you both learn knowledgeable ways to accomplish a task or use resources. As a gold duo, your love of life attracts loads of friends. Your creative, nonstop-fun approach to tasks can turn even the mundane into a party.

Relationship Tips

Though each of you has a different vision, keep your relationship fun by appreciating how the other does his own thing. Delight in your partner's inventiveness. But don't exclude others from your overall scheme, or you may become somewhat disengaged. Be cautious when you take on the same task together, as competitive issues may deplete your efforts.

PART FOUR

SYNCHRONICITY

Creating One Vision Through Color

CHAPTER SEVENTEEN

Color by Color

Living with the Dewey Color System®

Appreciation is a wonderful thing. It makes what is excellent in others belong to us as well.

—Voltaire

Genuine appreciation is the key to happiness. Rejoice together, as the wonderful things that you already know about each other—but sometimes just forget to observe—are again revealed. In this chapter, as you revisit each color's gifts, you'll be reminded of just how special you both are to each other.

CELEBRATE EACH OTHER'S GIFTS

Letters, e-mails, and workshop conversations from our readers are included in this chapter. Though names have been changed, their responses tell firsthand what it's like living with the Dewey Color System. Each illustrates an understanding of their own and their partner's self-truths. What can you learn from these stories? By embracing the full spectrum of knowledge about each other, you gain a powerful, close-knit relationship connection.

Each of the fifteen colors represents an amazing gift. Consider, as you go, how you both ranked your color choices. Be affirmed by your first choices, proud of your empowering second choices, and in full support of your third choices.

> *If we have no peace, it is because we have forgotten that we belong to each other.*
> —MOTHER TERESA

THE 15 GREAT GIFTS

Lime Green	The Gift of Self-Reflection
Green	The Gift of Being Comfortable with Yourself
Teal	The Gift of Believing in Your Wishes
Blue	The Gift of Crafting a Beautiful Future
Indigo	The Gift of Turning Thought into Action
Purple	The Gift of Knowing Your Greatness
Magenta	The Gift of Optimism
Red	The Gift of Finding Your Voice
Red-Orange	The Gift of Expressing Your Heart
Orange	The Gift of Realistic Expectations
Gold	The Gift of Passionate Living
Yellow	The Gift of Keeping Your Power
Black	The Gift of Knowing Your Heart
White	The Gift of Beginning Anew
Brown	The Gift of Living an Authentic Life

Lime Green: The Gift of Self-Reflection

When you feel let down, lied to, or frustrated, look again. Bluntly question your frustrations. Carefully weigh how you feel and don't allow any other considerations. Pertinent information will flood your mind with understanding that positively alters your point of view. You'll feel more alive, impassioned with goals and desires.

> *Whenever you question the uncomfortable areas of your thoughts, you awaken your desires.*

BRENDA'S STORY

A conversation between two sisters. One, who loves lime green, is being driven crazy by phone calls from the other, who disdains lime green.

"My sister, who doesn't like lime green, was driving me crazy, asking questions over and over that she should have already known the answers to. As always, I asked, 'What's the problem?' and she, as always, responded, 'Nothing, really.' Which is the story of her life—always avoiding. Then, after a moment of silence, she says, 'My boyfriend's only calling me once a day.' I replied, 'For God's sake, maybe he's just busy!'

"As usual, I had to intercede. 'Instead of whining about this, why don't you talk to him about it?' She said, 'I would, but I don't want him to think that I'm high maintenance.' 'Well,' I told her, 'if you don't, you're going to have a fight, or maybe end the relationship like you always do.'"

LIME GREEN AND YOU

Lime green gives you the stamina to question what's missing in your life. Ignite your passions by letting your inner voice speak. You will discover how you are yearning to feel.

Questioning yourself gives you the power to know exactly what you need to do.

The more you like lime green, the more you question what is missing in your life.

The less you like lime green, the more you avoid confronting what is missing in your life.

Exploring your thoughts is not the same as embracing them. Don't be afraid to confess your hidden, shocking considerations. They are simply clues to understanding yourself.

Green: The Gift of Being Comfortable with Yourself

When you're relaxed, consider what you need. Then tell your partner how he can best support you. Clarity will turn issues that appeared complicated into "aha" moments. You'll find yourself saying, "Oh, we should have done that long ago." Not having to second-guess what your partner needs will make your lives together less stressful.

> *Whenever you confess to yourself what you want,
> others feel comfortable.*

LINDA'S STORY

A busy career mom who is a first-choice green talks about being married to a third-choice green.

"You would think that when a man has a headache he would know to take something. My husband, who's a third-choice green, will work in the dark until I turn the lights on for him. Even though he's completely dedicated to taking care of us, he just doesn't know how to take care of himself.

"Yes, it's as if I have another kid. And without a doubt, I'm overwhelmed at times. Knowing, however, that he just can't help it makes me okay with being there for him. Gosh knows he's always in full support of me. Thankfully, my mother-in-law, my closest ally, helps a lot. Otherwise, I'd crash and burn."

GREEN AND YOU

Green gives you a stronger understanding of yourself. Be true to the child in you. Take the time to make sure that the "me" in you is okay. You will obtain the power of inner strength and be able to create a more nurturing, supportive world.

The more you like green, the more aware you are of the support that you and others need.

The less you like green, the more difficult it is to be aware, within yourself, of what you need.

Visit with the very real you by forgetting, for the moment, your career and others' needs. Just be with your thoughts. Listen and your inner voice will tell you what you require to be comfortable. Your greater awareness will detect what's needed.

Teal: The Gift of Believing in Your Wishes

Today, in our sophisticated world, we have so many choices that wishing for meaningful things is essential. A career that you love and a relationship that will grow closer and closer are a few suggestions to get you started. Wishes will give you both the clarity to focus on winning futures.

Whenever you make others a winner, you win, too.

MEGAN'S STORY

A low-preference teal is surrounded by many high-preference teal friends.

"I've recently discovered that most of my friends love teal. Just like your book said, hanging around [teals] makes me believe that I can do anything that I want to do. But I hate the idea that I need all that flattery; knowing that I need their compliments! Still, don't get me wrong. I'd do anything to help my friends. I couldn't manage without them."

TEAL AND YOU

Teal inspires you to believe in your aspirations. Get intense. Wish over and over until you believe in your capacity to accomplish your dreams. Believe in your wish and you will gain the power to believe in yourself.

The more you like teal, the more you believe that you and others can attain your dreams.

The less you like teal, the more difficult it is for you to believe that you are capable of achieving your dreams.

Don't judge yourself by who you are now. You are not your job, the ex–homecoming queen, the star athlete, or the math scholar. You are also who you dream to be! Ask others about their dreams. Now close your eyes and visualize your own dreams. Become inspired.

Blue: The Gift of Crafting a Beautiful Future

Concentrate on the great gifts that you both contribute to each other. Don't get caught up in your appearances, which are different, or even each other's weird quirks. They're all deceiving. If you see your partner, instead, for his contributions to your relationship, you will open each other's hearts and minds.

> *Whenever you perceive positive things about others, they see your point of view.*

JODI'S STORY

A top sales rep who's a third-choice blue is in conflict with her bosses (two first-choice blues). Recall that a third-choice blue's honesty is unparalleled and can be viewed, especially by a first-choice blue, as a personal attack.

"I just got fired, [even though] I'm the number one sales rep for the entire division. I was told that I was just not a team player. We had been going through lots of changes at work and my two first-choice-blue managers kept asking me, 'What do you think?' So I told them.

"Apparently, they just wanted me to agree with whatever they said. Why'd they ask if they didn't want to know? But the joke's on them now. Their top competitor just hired me!"

BLUE AND YOU

Blue gives you the focus to visualize. Expand your mind by concentrating on your future. Dream. You will gain the power of mental discipline and be able to envision a more beautiful life.

The more you like blue, the more optimistic you are that your dreams will work.

The less you like blue, the more pessimistic you are that your dreams will work.

Make a definite goal. Regularly assessing your future will keep you on the right road. Focus, focus, focus. Do not relent until you become your aspiration. Others will see your courage as self-confidence and want to be on your team.

Indigo: The Gift of Turning Thought into Action

Decide in advance what you and your partner will do together. Before you start a project, particularly in a workplace setting, discuss in detail what could go wrong. Then take action. You get excited by planning ahead, and your desires fuel success.

> *Whenever you make an exciting plan, you create success.*

LAURA'S STORY

A first-choice indigo is experiencing her first Christmas with her third-choice-indigo mother-in-law. In reading about a low-preference indigo, she learned how to go with the flow.

"My new husband and I had so many places to go that I needed a way to keep everything straight. So I made a travel plan, just like I always do around the holidays. Then I e-mailed it to my mother-in-law, making sure, of course, that we were arriving exactly when she wanted us to be there.

"Then I got this really out-there phone call from her. I couldn't believe it. Laughing, she said, 'You goof, don't ever do that to me again!' So as you can imagine, I'm wondering what the heck is she talking about.

"Come to find out, she just doesn't like to make plans—at all. And it's not just at Christmas—never! She drives me nuts. My husband thinks it's all a scream. And I must admit that it's entertaining, since things somehow always work out."

INDIGO AND YOU

Indigo gives you an enlightened perspective to create successful plans. Delve into each ingredient you might need to create your idea. You will gain the power to orchestrate your future.

The more you like indigo, the more you enjoy making plans and conceptualizing new ideas.

The less you like indigo, the harder it is for you to feel that you need to make a plan.

Establish an unrelenting focus by zeroing in on exactly how you can accomplish your goals. Keep lists. Dedicate your thoughts to clarifying why you need to do each thing. Are there any shortcuts? Now, redo your original plan by adopting better or easier ways.

Purple: The Gift of Knowing Your Greatness

Take the time to get beyond the surface—recognize and confront the "why" of every issue. In turn, you'll gain the ability to craft winning strategies and better understand your own potential. Even though preconceived opinions sometimes allow you to get things done faster, they're dangerous. Not fully knowing the facts of a situation is like waiting for a bomb to explode.

Whatever you dwell on, for better or worse, creates possibilities.

DEWEY'S STORY

I love purple! Here's a story about how my high preference for purple got me into trouble with clients.

"When I owned a staffing company, I trained hundreds of sales representatives. Most of them preferred purple—just as I do. Driving back from sales calls, we 'purples' would sometimes make assumptions about what the client needed, instead of later asking them directly.

"One of us would say, for example, 'Do you think that we need to charge $8 an hour for that skill?' Then the other one would reply something like 'No, let's charge $8.20 an hour.'

"But our know-it-all approach occasionally got us into trouble. In this case, our assumed price structure lost us an account—and we realized it too late. If we had only asked the client up front, we could have won them over."

PURPLE AND YOU

Purple creates the ability to see new possibilities, ideas, and strategies for yourself and others. Visit with your emotions. In them, you'll discover a greatness that can only be imagined. You and your partner will gain the personal power to create something original.

The more you like purple, the more prone you are to self-assurance, contemplation, and self-examination.

The less you like purple, the more likely you are to deny your capabilities.

Fight for what you believe. Don't be in a rush. Imagine that you have five years to accomplish your goals. Now, what are the possibilities? Get emotional. Address your limitations beforehand, so that you'll have no reservations about what you need to do. Then charge ahead with all your heart.

Magenta: The Gift of Optimism

Smile and the world smiles with you. Without your saying a word, others will respond positively to you. What you feel is what you get. So, work it! Create appeal with your tone of voice and body language, as these speak louder than words. You'll attract great opportunities for love and success.

Whatever you feel enthusiastic about creates opportunities.

DAVID'S STORY

A low-preference magenta is writing about his first-choice-magenta boss.

"My boss loves magenta. And just like you state, she is constantly starting projects around the office. She's one nonstop, inspirational powerhouse and it's driving all of us absolutely nuts.

"Not only are we working like crazy all day, she's also gotten us involved in community activities that have swallowed our evenings. But now we've learned how to defend ourselves. When she starts pushing our hot buttons, we let her know right away, 'You're not tricking us!'

"In her defense, however, she's also somehow gotten me married, and talked me into having kids. So in some ways, she's been my angel, too."

MAGENTA AND YOU

Magenta inspires you to start something new. Conjure up a curious, adventurous spirit. Get enthusiastic about doing something or being with someone by considering how much fun it could be. The world will open up to you.

The more you like magenta, the more you are inspired by your environment.

The less you like magenta, the more suspicious you are of change.

Here's how to create a spark in your life: start by discarding your skeptical thoughts. Focus instead on how exciting a person or place could be. Allow your curiosity and the quest for something entirely new to rule the moment. Your exciting new body language will attract whatever you desire.

Red: The Gift of Finding Your Voice

Protect yourself. Before you invest your time, make sure that others' requests include your heartfelt concerns as well. Examine their motivations, set firm boundaries, and enforce self-protective rules to create a life that works best for you.

Whenever you express what's needed, others can give support.

JENNIFER'S STORY

A third-choice red comments on how her mom, a first-choice red, taught her how to speak up for herself.

"As a child, the very thought of even complaining to a waiter about a mistake in my order scared me to death! Seriously, I'd rather just not eat.

"So, I'd complain about the bad food to my mom right away, expecting her to make it right. But she just wouldn't stand for that. Instead, she'd tell me what to say and wouldn't back off until I spoke up.

"Even today, it still takes a conscious effort for me to speak up. Somehow, when the wrong order arrives, I hear her voice and back it goes! My husband makes jokes about how I've become my mom, even sound like her when I give orders. But that's okay with me."

RED AND YOU

Red gives you the practical knowledge and expressive power to direct your life. Speak up. Tell the world who you are and what you want. You will gain the power to make your life and things around you work.

The more you like red, the less tolerance you have for failure or incompetence.

The less you like red, the more you will tolerate things that you do not enjoy.

Be specific. Let others know what they can expect from you. Tell them about your strengths, weaknesses, and exactly what you need. Tell your boss that you can do your job, and tell your partner what you need to be happier. Your world will become more about what you require to be a success.

Red-Orange: The Gift of Expressing Your Heart

Never be indifferent. Everyone deserves genuine respect. You can avoid upsets, for the most part, by recognizing your partner's heartfelt contributions to your life. Hold one another in high esteem and even the toughest situations will be forgiven.

> *Whatever you say from your heart is heard as a concern.*

ROBYN'S STORY

A woman who loves red-orange is upset with her best friend's new low-preference-red-orange husband.

"My best friend just got married to a much older guy. I wasn't surprised at all, when I did their colors, to see that he dislikes red-orange. At parties, in particular, he's constantly taking the focus off of her so that people won't pause and notice their age difference.

"He's so afraid that his buddies are going to see him as robbing the cradle. It especially upsets me when he introduces her not as his wife, but simply by her first name. It saddens me when she's treated as unimportant. I wish he would get it. She really loves him."

RED-ORANGE AND YOU

Red-orange gives you the self-respect to honor your individuality. Look people in the eye when you speak. Appreciate what they do for you. Honor those who love and respect you, and you will gain the power to honor yourself.

The more you like red-orange, the more you honor your individuality.

The less you like red-orange, the more difficult it is for you to distinguish yourself from society.

Make time for whoever or whatever is important to you. Your focused efforts will get things done and show others how much you care. Consider the people and issues you think about the most. Aren't they the most important in your life?

Orange: The Gift of Realistic Expectations

Ask yourself and your partner probing questions. Be courageous. Confront whatever makes you feel frustrated or out on a limb. By doing so, you can turn your dreams, and even situations you're worried about, into obtainable plans and fulfilling moments.

> *Whenever you create reasonable expectations, you can win.*

SHAWNA'S STORY

A third-choice orange is being proposed to by a first-choice orange.

"There I was in the beautiful Napa Valley with the man of my dreams and, to be quite honest, hoping with all my heart that he would propose. Instead, from nowhere, I got twenty nonstop questions. 'If we get married, can we live in my house or does it have to be yours? Do you really need to have children right away or can we wait for a while?' And so they went. My mood was spoiled.

"Then I remembered this was just an orange thing—that they ask loads of questions before saying yes to anything. Romantic, yuck, are you kidding? I just hated it. But at least I was at peace knowing that this was his way, [that it wasn't] about me. Oh yeah, then he actually got down on his knee and gave me the perfect ring."

ORANGE AND YOU

Orange makes positive change easier for you. It enables you to disassociate from what you expect from yourself to realize the clarity of a situation. You gain the power to eliminate or change the direction of dead-end situations and relationships.

The more you like orange, the easier it is for you to disassociate from your expectations to see the truth of a situation.

The less you like orange, the more you tend to expect from yourself—more than you can deliver.

Underpromise and overdeliver. Reevaluate your expectations of yourself and others frequently. When you find yourself working harder or feeling too serious, ask those around you, "Exactly how do you picture this situation?" Everyone will be happier, especially you, when you're realistic and up-front about what you can do.

Gold: The Gift of Passionate Living

Jettison the to-do list items and daily agendas that aren't worth your time. It can be tough, especially if you're used to being perpetually "busy," but let them go. When free time and space surround you, you'll feel a burst of passion. What you desire most will take center stage. You'll find that something you truly love will replace these nagging, undesirable situations.

> *Whatever feels desirable creates passion.*

SHARON'S STORY

A recently retired low-preference-gold woman is freaking out because she has too much time on her hands.

"As a person who really doesn't like the color gold, it really hit a nerve with me when I read about it in your book. At first, I got upset and thought the description was wrong. After all, everyone will tell you that I'm a fun person. But then, as I read further, I realized that I had misunderstood. It was more about the fact that I can't stop thinking about what to do. And boy is that my issue!

"I have to consciously make myself relax. Right now, even though I have nothing to do, I'm somehow overwhelmed. I've been crazy-busy doing stupid stuff. It really helped reading your book. Now I'm going to end my nonstop thinking. I want things to be fun for me, too."

GOLD AND YOU

Gold gives you the power to rediscover what gives you pleasure. Ignite your inner fire. Simply give yourself time to do what feels good. Stop thinking so much, and the world around you will become an adventurous playground.

The more you like gold, the more you know how to use your resources to create new things.

The less you like gold, the more your undesirable thoughts distract you from knowing what makes you passionate.

Take out the trash—things you don't enjoy. Your new, carefree, more passionate perspective will convey confidence and attract friends and business. Always doing what you are supposed to be doing will run your battery down. Make your energy zoom by doing what your heart desires.

Yellow: The Gift of Keeping Your Power

Taking to heart others' insensitive words or feeling obligated to conform to someone else's agenda can destroy your will to be yourself. Don't give up your power. Know that what other people do is primarily about them, not you.

> *Whenever someone speaks, see his or her point of view.*

GREG'S STORY

A third-choice-yellow teenager is rebelling against his dad, a first-choice yellow.

"Whenever my dad tried to tell me something, I resented it. I used to get upset and blast him with 'Thank you, but I can take care of myself!' I knew exactly what I wanted and his suggestions just got in the way. It was like he thought I couldn't do anything without him.

"Now that I've done his colors, I get it. Things are different. He's a yellow, a guy who has to pay attention to things. Guess I can learn from that. The war is over. We don't fight anymore."

YELLOW AND YOU

Yellow gives you the wisdom to know what's needed. Constantly critique the ongoing conversation you're having with yourself by reevaluating what you're getting from people and situations. You will gain the power to distinguish your own needs and realistically appraise others' concerns without bias.

The more you like yellow, the more willing you are to get information before coming to conclusions.

The less you like yellow, the sooner you come to a conclusion, even if you have not heard all the facts.

Don't waste your time on something you cannot change or someone who doesn't know what he wants. Each person or situation is in a particular state for a reason. Accept that and move on to what fits your sensibility or to the people who will support you the most.

Black: The Gift of Knowing Your Heart

Who do you have relationships with right now? Aren't these the same people who support your future? Express your love and concern, and they will give back the same. Tell them what's so wonderful about them, and you'll experience the magic of appreciation.

Whatever makes you feel good, hold on to dearly.

JONATHAN'S STORY

A first-choice black is upset with his third-choice-black boss. Consider how unnecessarily hurt feelings have intruded on their ability to communicate.

"In reading your book, it was a relief to learn my boss, a third-choice black, can't hear emotion. *Insensitive* was the word that I always used to describe her. Yes, notably, I do get all wrapped up in my own feelings. It's just who I am, especially when office politics makes my day hell.

"Your explanation that she just can't hear what's said with emotions has helped me. I thought that she was ignoring me. And yeah, I'm working on calming myself down before I ask for help. Thanks for the tip. My voice, evidently, is loaded with emotion."

BLACK AND YOU

Black gives you the courage to know your own emotions. Take the plunge. Feel both your pleasant and your painful experiences, but don't obsess over them. You will experience the power of genuine appreciation for yourself and others.

The more you like black, the more you are ruled by your emotions.

The less you like black, the more you avoid your emotions.

Emotions, like it or not, determine your thoughts and eventually your actions. Thoughts such as "Everything about that person [or situation] is perfect" or "Is life worth living?" are warning signs that you're avoiding a self-truth. Get real. Don't obsess over how you feel.

White: The Gift of Beginning Anew

When you find yourself not being objective—stop. Consider where else you can go to get what you need. Many times this is the question that friends or family can best answer. Put an end to what's not working and don't worry. A solution will arrive.

*Whenever something ends, always believe something
new will begin.*

DARLENE'S STORY

*A wife who's a first-choice white is writing about her husband, a
first-choice black.*

"My husband, who's a first-choice black, has opinions
about everything. He knows exactly what he wants before he's
thought things through. After twenty-five years of marriage, I
find his entire routine hilarious.

"Guess that I've finally figured things out, even before I
read your book. I simply hear his opinion and wait until the
next day to offer a suggestion. After his emotions have subsided,
for the most part, I can do exactly what I want to do."

WHITE AND YOU

White gives you the objectivity to see all your available
options. Step back and view your world as if you were not a
part of it. In keeping your distance, you'll gain the power to
decipher new opportunities for yourself and those you love.

The more you like white, the faster you are able to shift gears
and explore new options.

The less you like white, the longer it takes you to break free
of problematic situations.

Ponder this question: In the entire world, if you could
have anything, what or who would it be? Now look at your
current relationships and circumstances and decide what you
need to change, request, keep, or let go.

Brown: The Gift of Living an Authentic Life

Keep your life rolling forward by accepting everything and everyone as they are right now. Don't let disappointments slow you down. Pause long enough to learn from them and don't let your defensiveness shut you down.

Whenever you accept situations without judgment, you evolve.

CAROL'S STORY

A first-choice brown discusses her frustration with her third-choice-brown neighbor.

"My next-door neighbor is an aging beauty queen. Don't get me wrong, she's still a beautiful woman. But recently, she's started dressing like a teenager—miniskirts and all! For heaven's sake, she's a grandmother.

"We're both retired and go shopping together. Now, however, I refuse to go unless she dresses her age. I just tell her up front that it makes me uncomfortable when everyone starts gawking at us. Of course, I still love her, and now that I know she hates brown, I understand her—silly looks and all."

BROWN AND YOU

Brown grounds you. Immerse yourself in understanding how others' experiences comprise their understanding of the world. Consider this before you judge a person or a situation. By doing so, you'll embrace life, people, and things as they are.

The more you like brown, the more aware you are of your environment and the temporary nature of life.

The less you like brown, the longer it takes you to recognize the realities of your environment and life itself.

Be real. Forget about power and status. The more airs you put on or the more you try to disguise your shortcomings, the more apparent they become. Become grounded by simply being yourself. Without illusions, your spirits will thrive on genuine appreciation.

ON A FINAL NOTE

View your life as plentiful. Say good morning to every person you love when you arise each day—even if they're not with you. Give thanks at night for what went well. Embrace everyone with smiles and genuine concern. Pure sunshine will envelop your heart and your world will spin back love, support, abundance, and success. Choose happiness.

> *Live. Live. Live. Life is a banquet and most poor suckers are starving to death.*
> —ROSALIND RUSSELL IN *AUNTIE MAME*

Relationships Color Categories

Name:

Color category selections:

CATEGORY	FIRST CHOICE	SECOND CHOICE	THIRD CHOICE
PRIMARY			
SECONDARY			
ACHROMATIC			

CATEGORY	BOX 1 First Choice	BOX 2 First Choice	BOX 3 First Choice
INTERMEDIATE			

Name:

Color category selections:

CATEGORY	FIRST CHOICE	SECOND CHOICE	THIRD CHOICE
PRIMARY			
SECONDARY			
ACHROMATIC			

CATEGORY	BOX 1 First Choice	BOX 2 First Choice	BOX 3 First Choice
INTERMEDIATE			

Name:

Color category selections:

CATEGORY	FIRST CHOICE	SECOND CHOICE	THIRD CHOICE
PRIMARY			
SECONDARY			
ACHROMATIC			

CATEGORY	BOX 1 First Choice	BOX 2 First Choice	BOX 3 First Choice
INTERMEDIATE			

Name:

Color category selections:

CATEGORY	FIRST CHOICE	SECOND CHOICE	THIRD CHOICE
PRIMARY			
SECONDARY			
ACHROMATIC			

CATEGORY	BOX 1 First Choice	BOX 2 First Choice	BOX 3 First Choice
INTERMEDIATE			

Name:

Color Category Selections:

CATEGORY	FIRST CHOICE	SECOND CHOICE	THIRD CHOICE
PRIMARY			
SECONDARY			
ACHROMATIC			

CATEGORY	BOX 1 First Choice	BOX 2 First Choice	BOX 3 First Choice
INTERMEDIATE			

Color Products Available from Energia Press

THE DEWEY COLOR COORDINATOR $28.00

Take this book with you when you're buying clothes or furnishings. At a glance you will see seventy-six colors that coordinate with your attire, furniture, or walls. Use this brilliant shopping guide to make your world more spiritual, sensual, and adventurous.

DEWEY COLOR KIDS $8.95

Give your child the gift of passionate, brilliant color. This interactive children's book for ages six months to eight years old will teach your child basic color and reading skills. Use it in conjunction with *The Dewey Color System®: Choose Your Colors, Change Your Life* to better understand how to be supportive without destroying your child's essence.

DEWEY COLOR CARDS $18.95

Inspire new perspectives with brilliant color in this array of fifteen magnificently printed greeting cards that share the powerful vibrations of color. Each card has a vellum envelope and an inspirational message. There is plenty of room to write your own message, too.

DEWEY COLOR PUZZLE $8.99

Put your color skills to the test. This fun, fast puzzle will challenge your ability to see color. Complete it in less than five minutes, and you are a chromatic expert. Practice makes perfect. Do it over and over to sharpen your visual color skills.

DEWEY COLOR CHAMELEONS $15.95

The Dewey Color Chameleon sports fifteen power-color shirts, and you will want to collect them all! Each color has its own meaning.

For the store nearest you, call 1-866-351-5001 or log on to our Web site, www.deweycolorsystem.com.

Check Out Our Web Site

Visit www.deweycolorsystem.com and obtain digital passion profiles. You can select personal printouts for yourself, or e-mail your friends and loved ones with a printout gift. Below is a sample profile list.

PERSONAL PROFILES

* Your Color Type: More Peace, More Happiness
* Hue Are You: More Insight, More Passion
* Relationships: More Love, More Sex
* Career: More Money, More Fun

SIX-MINUTE PERSONALITY TEST

Instead of the industry average of over two hours, the system predicts, in six minutes, sixteen personality factors, occupational interests, coping skills, and interpersonal interaction style. It can also establish for each individual his or her preferred organizational style, leadership role, and work setting. With so much data available, human resource departments can now pick from a menu to establish customized criteria.

CAREER COUNSELING FOR THE CLUELESS

The system statistically predicts, without the bias factor of language, occupations that create personal fulfillment and success. For example, is mathematics, medical science, art, writing, public speaking, law, sales, or organizational management the best profession for you? Those struggling for insight will learn about the best career for them.

Order a profile, a copy of *The Dewey Color System®: Choose Your Colors, Change Your Life,* and much more directly from our Web site, or write to: Energia, Inc., P.O. Box 669306, Marietta, Georgia 30066.

ACKNOWLEDGMENTS

My thanks to:

Dewey Sadka Sr., my dad, for his unrelenting faith in my ability.

Jennifer Burris, my apprentice and vice president of product development, for eleven years of complete devotion to making this system available as a new resource for the world.

Roberto Athayde, for exposing me to a world that inspired my creation.

Mary Ann Petro, for her brilliant, knowledgeable perspectives on color and design.

Queenie Sadka Nassour, for showing me the power of passionate love.

Lillie Mae Sams, for twenty-six years of love and concern.

Ellis Nassour, for his editing insights and for keeping this project on track.

Jerry Henderson, for leading me through the tough times.

Dr. Don Davis, for his life-altering, inspirational support.

Antonis Ampatzis and Dr. Jerry Gardner for the great gift of friendship.

ABOUT THE AUTHOR

DEWEY SADKA is the founder of one of the largest employment agencies in the country. A veteran user of traditional tools like the Myers-Briggs test, he longed for a system that would bypass the limitations of language in traditional but imprecise questionnaires and truly reveal skills and limitations. Long fascinated with color and the science behind it, Dewey created his system. Now it's the world's first valid color-based personality test and is available to human resource professionals and clinical psychologists worldwide. The Dewey Color System has been featured on the Discovery Channel's *Christopher Lowell Show,* on CNN, on National Public Radio, and in the *Wall Street Journal,* the *Chicago Tribune,* the *Washington Post, Better Homes and Gardens, Metropolitan Home, Elle—Canada, Cosmopolitan, Women's Day, Woman's World,* and more than forty other national magazines. Mr. Sadka conducts diversity training for major corporations and career seminars for universities, and lectures on how to best use color in design for associations and conventions. He resides in Atlanta.

Learn the basics of the
Dewey Color System

Are you a red–orange–black? A yellow–green–white? Or a blue–green–brown? The Dewey Color System is a fun, interactive self-test based on the concept that your favorite colors reflect the core of your personality—your hopes and aspirations—and your least favorite colors represent areas for improvement.

The Dewey Color System
1-4000-5062-6
$14.00 paper (Canada: $21.00)